INTIMATE DECEPTION

Escaping the Trap of Sexual Impurity

P. ROGER HILLERSTROM

MULTN OMAH

PORTLAND, OREGON 97266

Names have been changed to protect the privacy of individuals mentioned in case studies.

Edited by Deena Davis
Cover design by Judy Quinn

INTIMATE DECEPTION
© 1989 by Multnomah Press
Portland, Oregon 97266

Multnomah Press is a ministry of Multnomah School of the Bible, 8435 N.E. Glisan Street, Portland, Oregon 97220

Printed in the United States of America

Library of Congress Cataloging-in-Publication Data

Hillerstrom, P. Roger.
  Intimate deception / P. Roger Hillerstrom.
    p.   cm.
  ISBN 0-88070-230-3
  1. Sexual ethics—United States. 2. Premarital sex—United States—Moral and ethical aspects. 3. Single people—United States—Sexual behavior—Moral and ethical aspects. 4. Sex—Religious aspects—Christianity. I. Title.
HQ32.H55 1988
306.7—dc19   88-38089
                                                                   CIP

94 95 – 10 9 8 7 6 5 4

INTIMATE
DECEPTION

To my wife Beth—
my chief editor, primary consultant,
"forever prayer partner," and best friend . . .
and to
my parents, Per and Gully Hillerstrom
who throughout my life have taught me in word and deed
the meaning of commitment and friendship in marriage

C O N T E N T S

FOREWORD

One of the many joys of teaching graduate school included meeting and teaching students with unusual talents and gifts. One of those students was Roger Hillerstrom, who is now a co-worker and therapist. His insights and concern for the practical are evident in this book. His content speaks directly to present-day concerns. This book is designed to be informative, to create personal reflection and discussion, and to lead the reader in the process of clarifying his or her own values as well as behavior.

Writing with clarity, Roger presents clear and concise illustrations with numerous interesting and helpful case studies. He is able to delicately balance confrontation of specific problems without being condemning or judgmental.

You will discover a new perspective on your own situation and that of others as you recognize the author's balanced emphasis on behavior as well as feelings—an emphasis that sets this book apart from other books on the subject. It is also a rich resource from which to draw teaching material.

Singles, marrieds, parents, ministers . . . yes, everyone can benefit from reading *Intimate Deception*.

H. Norman Wright, Director
Family Counseling and Enrichment
Santa Ana, California

PREFACE

I am a family therapist, a marriage counselor. The content of this book has developed from my experience in working with troubled married couples as well as unmarried couples who are preparing for marriage commitment.

For several years, I have observed patterns in these relationships that seemed so clear and so predictable that I was surprised I had never read about them. The professional literature seemed to ignore them, and the popular literature seemed unaware of them. I began teaching about these patterns in counselor training seminars and always received extremely positive responses.

I then wrote a brief article regarding these patterns. I was astounded by the response. It has been published several times and requests for copies have come in by the thousands. Almost four years later, I am still getting responses to that article. People make comments such as, "It's like you've been looking into our private lives!"

and "This is written about us" and "Suddenly our problems make sense."

I still find very little written about these patterns, although their effects on marriage are profound. However, the effects need not be overwhelming if couples are willing to face them and make changes.

Though I've tried to keep this book from being offensively explicit, this is not a book for children. It is written to adults who desire to improve their relationships. For those who are unmarried, its purpose is to help them develop healthy relationships in which emotional intimacy can grow and flourish. For married couples, its goal is to restore and rebuild relationships that have been damaged by poor decisions regarding sexuality. For parents, pastors, and youth leaders, it can be used as a tool in dealing with the questions, concerns, and fears of young people in a society that has profoundly confused the purpose of sexual relationships.

As you read this book, my prayer is that you will find direction and motivation to make some positive changes in your closest relationships.

A WORD OF THANKS

I am deeply aware that this book is not the result of my work alone. It is a composite of many minds, personalities, and lifetimes. My life has been filled with people who have influenced every page. To each and every one I owe a debt of gratitude.

A word of thanks . . .

to my wife Beth, who did everything from editing manuscripts to keeping the kids out of my hair while I wrote.

to H. Norman Wright, who nudged me into this project and whose role of teacher and mentor in my life is more significant than he realizes.

to Genevieve Bell, a remarkable lady whose grasp of the English language has, in six months, made up for twelve years of poor English teaching. (As well as twelve years of goofing off in class!)

Acknowledgments

to Kin Millen, whose insight and experience shaped the proposal of this book.

to Kirk Farnsworth and the staff of Crista Counseling Service for their support and encouragement. In particular:

Dr. Grant Martin, who saved me years of mistakes through sharing his own writing and publishing experience;

Dr. Claude McCoy, for the encouragement and accountability of my Wednesday morning "kick in the pants";

Dr. Mike Rattray, whose computer helped save my time and my mind;

Dr. Reed Davis, who helped edit the original manuscript;

Jean Lush, for her confidence in my ability as an author. She taught me so much from both her successes and mistakes.

to Eldon Berg, one of the world's few computer geniuses who speaks my language. Without him, I'd still be scribbling.

to my other "computer tutors," Dave Crombie, Larry Plett, and Dave Reeber. Their knowledge and experience helped soothe my paranoia of the dreaded "machine."

to our Tuesday evening Bible study group for their constant encouragement, prayer support, and comic relief.

to Reverend Jan David Hettinga, who has served as a sounding board for my theology more than once.

to several couples whose encouragement, creativity, insight, and friendship helped shape the manuscript: Mark and Andrea Robertson, Jeff and Lynn Robson,

Robb and Cindy Swenson, Paul and Teresa Baldwin, and Rich and Jinny Liljenberg.

to Deena Davis and the staff of Multnomah Press for their contagious enthusiasm and hard work.

to my parents, Per and Gully Hillerstrom, and Beth's parents, Erwin and Betty Neese, for their belief in me, excited encouragement, and prayer support.

to my children, Karlyn and Luke, for their sincere cooperation with "Daddy's book."

to my neighbors and many other friends who are a source of encouragement and support to me—my thanks to you all!

There is a safety code built into us by our Manufacturer that is designed for maximum performance with minimum malfunction, especially in the area of sexual relationships.

1

THE BALANCING ACT

———————————————————————————

"You're the one who's crazy!" Susan was obviously angry and offended by the discussion with her father. "Just because I happen to enjoy being intimate doesn't mean my psyche is messed up. I think you're the one who needs a shrink! Sex is nothing more than two caring people touching each other; as long as both people enjoy it and no one gets hurt, there's nothing wrong with it. It's beautiful and clean and good. It's people like you who make sex dirty!"

Susan's father had brought his attractive nineteen-year-old daughter into my office for psychological evaluation. His concern stemmed from her sexual promiscuity. He leaned back in his chair, staring intensely at his daughter. "This whole conversation is disgusting! The Bible tells us to not even talk about such things. When I was your age I had never even imagined the things you're doing. No one had heard of herpes or AIDS. Men and women could fall in love without behaving like animals."

His voice lowered to almost a whisper, "The world was a better place then."

The differences in sexual attitudes in our culture are amazing! Often parents and their children disagree so drastically in their views that there is no apparent room for compromise. Even within the same generation we see huge differences in values, opinions, and practices. The very nature and purpose of the sexual relationship seems unclear at times, resulting in confusion and estrangement for countless individuals.

So What's New?

This conflict and confusion may seem like a product of the "now" generation, but that's far from the truth. It's been going on for centuries, and history shows us that the pendulum of sexual values has been swinging for some time. The prim Victorian era of the late nineteenth century reflected one extreme. In those days the fear of sensuality and sinful behavior ran so high that it brought about a custom of sewing covers for table legs. It was thought that the sight of a leg, even a table leg, might stimulate lustful thoughts!

That era gave way to the "Roaring Twenties." This was a period of indulgence, economically as well as morally. Women raised their skirts, cut their hair, and smoked cigarettes. Talking about sex and writing books about sex were no longer taboo. Sexual freedom was "in."

The thirties brought us the Great Depression, and with it a resurgence of conservative values. Sexual attitudes became less and less a topic of conversation. "Taboo" was back in style.

It wasn't until the "Baby Boom" of the late forties and early fifties that the pendulum began to swing the other direction again. The war was over, the economy was looking better, and the Kinsey Report brought sex back to the spotlight.

During the sixties and seventies, rock 'n' roll, hippies, and the playboy philosophy had a heyday. *Grass, acid,* and *free love* were common terms, along with *burned out, overdose,* and *VD.*

Each time the pendulum swings, it swings a little further and stays there a little longer, and with each extreme there are negative consequences for individuals as well as for all of society.

THE GOOD OLD DAYS

I've talked with many people of all ages who grew up in an era or a home environment that reflected sex as inherently evil. Often viewed by women of many generations as an unpleasant experience required of wives for their husbands, sexual intercourse has also been considered by some Christian groups to be an act distasteful to God but necessary for procreation. And some Christians even assume that sex must be a result of the Fall of Adam and Eve, therefore making it something to be strictly controlled by God through multiple regulations, commandments, and penalties. The influence of that atmosphere is still strong in many families today.

The results of this perspective are predictable. We would expect it to foster fears and anxieties about sexual behavior. We would expect people to be uncomfortable discussing sex or discussing problems involved in sexual relationships. Guilt and confusion about sex would probably be the most common experience of all.

Fear, anxiety, guilt, and *confusion* are terms that describe the sexual atmosphere of previous generations, and to some degree, segments of this generation. But the pendulum has not stopped swinging.

THE NEW "SOLUTION"?

The current swing of the sexual pendulum seems to reflect and encourage the opposite perspective of previous generations. Television shows promote it, commercials advertise it, Hollywood glamorizes it, parents tolerate it, and churches ignore it; what a combination! *Time* magazine reports:

> Like it or not, American adolescents are far more sexually active than they used to be. Guttmacher (Institute) statistics show that the incidence of sexual intercourse among unmarried teenage women increased by two-thirds during the 1970s. Moreover the sexual revolution seems to have moved from the college campus to the high school and now to the junior high and grade school. A 1982 survey conducted by Johns Hopkins researchers John Kanter and Melvin Zelnick found that nearly one out of five 15-year-old girls admitted that she had already had intercourse, as did nearly a third of 16-year-olds and 43% of 17-year-olds. "In the eyes of their peers, it is important for kids to be sexually active. No one wants to be a virgin," observes Amy Williams, director of San Francisco's Teen-age Pregnancy and Parenting Project (TAPP). The social pressure even on the youngest adolescents can be daunting. Says Stephany, 14, of suburban Chicago, now the mother of a four-month-old, "Everyone is like, 'did you lose your virginity yet?'"
>
> Social workers are almost unanimous in citing the influence of the popular media—television, rock music, videos, movies—in propelling the trend toward precocious sexuality. One survey has shown that in the course of a year the average viewer sees more than 9,000 scenes of suggested sexual intercourse or innuendo on prime time TV. "Our young people are barraged by the message that to be sophisticated they must be sexually hip." Says Williams, "They don't even buy toothpaste to clean their teeth. They buy it to be sexually attractive."[1]

In this morally relaxed atmosphere, we could expect sex

to become separated from commitment so that premarital sex would appear normal and healthy. We could expect epidemics of venereal diseases such as syphilis, gonorrhea, genital herpes, AIDS—and these do exist at alarming rates through every level of society. We could expect a plague of unwanted pregnancies, illegitimate children, and unwed teenage mothers. We could also expect a crisis over the issue of abortion, which too often is a desire to destroy the children produced as a result of sexual irresponsibility. An article published in *People* magazine described the sexual crisis this way:

> We are finding things out about teen sex faster than we ever wanted to. In 1985, prompted in part by news of a Chicago high school where a third of the female students were pregnant, the press aired some extremely unsettling facts. In America 3,000 adolescents become pregnant each day. A million a year. Four out of five are unmarried. More than half get abortions. "Babies having babies." Or killing them. Dismay turned to a deep fear a bit later, with recognition of the combined possibilities of adolescent sexuality and AIDS. Suddenly, the grim ante had been raised. Now our children's promiscuity could mean more than pregnancy—it could mean death.[2]

Many of the results are not so obvious. As a family therapist, I regularly see the effects of our society's attitude toward premarital sex—usually years later and most often in marriages. There is lack of intimacy, lack of trust, communication problems, sexual dysfunctions . . . the list goes on and on. These all stem from an act our society encourages in many ways.

But we are just now beginning to see a new soberness toward sexual promiscuity. In light of disease epidemics and spiritual, emotional, and relational emptiness, many people are ready for the pendulum to move once again.

WHERE DO WE GO FROM HERE?

I believe that both viewpoints—sexual laxity and sexual rigidity—are distortions of the truth. They are overreactions based in ignorance which result in serious and unnecessary consequences. Neither viewpoint is an accurate reflection of God's intention for the sexual relationship, or a reasonable understanding of what the Bible teaches about sex.

Years ago I heard Bob Vernon, Deputy Chief of Police for the Los Angeles Police Department, share his perspective on the Christian life. One illustration he gave related to the police cars used in the highway division. These are incredibly fast vehicles whose engines have been "altered" from the standard factory specifications. A logical concern would be their mechanical safety. Since they are driven hard, fast, and often, something must keep them from blowing up. Vernon explained that before the mechanics alter the engines, they contact the manufacturers—the people who originally designed and produced the car. The police department's mechanics learn from them the absolute maximum stress load the car's engine can handle for maximum performance without danger.

The function of Scripture in our lives is very similar to contacting the auto manufacturer in Bob's example. The author of the Bible is our designer and creator. He knows how we operate. He also knows how we can get maximum satisfaction and enjoyment out of these bodies with the fewest malfunctions.

The admonitions in God's word are focused toward that goal. God does not generally elaborate on the reasoning behind His commandments but His message is simply, *"Obey for an abundant life."*

Whenever we ignore a clear, direct command in the Bible we set a "trap" for ourselves that will eventually ensnare us. Regardless of how we rationalize or justify our behavior, or how many people we can convince that our behavior is right, the Bible says there is a safety code built into us by our Manufacturer designed for maximum performance with minimum malfunction, especially in the area of sexual relationships. We just can't change that.

Today many young Christian couples are asking very important questions about their sexual relationships:

"Isn't God more interested in love and relationship than a marriage license?"

"Since we are committed to each other, why wait for a piece of paper?"

"Why not 'practice' our sexual response to each other just like we practice other things before marriage, such as communication and decision making?"

"Isn't it rigid and legalistic to adhere to a set of ethics from a totally different culture and context than our own?"

"Since we love each other and we will get married, isn't that what really matters?"

These are questions that deserve answers, and they, as well as many others, will be answered in the following chapters.

This is a book of "traps"—the traps involved in violating God's structure for our sexual functioning. The more fully we understand them, the more easily we can avoid them. We will explore these traps from the fields of psychology, sociology, and medicine. We will also examine what the Bible teaches about our use of the gift of sex. Finally, we will explore ways of avoiding these traps, and if already caught, how to climb out of them.

I have provided a section at the end of each chapter titled "Growing Closer." The purpose of this section is to help the reader recognize, evaluate, and avoid potential "traps" associated with intimate relationships, as well as to provide guidelines for developing true intimacy through communication.

GROWING CLOSER

1	2	3	4	5	6	7	8	9	10
conservative									liberal

1) Place an "X" above the number representing where you think you are on a continuum between extremely liberal and extremely conservative in sexual attitudes.

2) Place an "A" above the number where you think most people in your age group are.

Are your feelings about the placement of your "X" more positive than negative, or vice versa?

How do you think your view of your peers affects where you placed yourself on the continuum?

3) What was the attitude toward sex in your parent's families?

4) How did that attitude influence the atmosphere in the home in which you grew up?

For those who are married:

5) How does that attitude influence your marriage and family life today?

Trying to experience marriage without a lifetime commitment is like going to a doughnut shop to buy your meals. You can fill your stomach, but eventually you'll die of malnutrition.

2

THE INTIMACY TRAP

"He lied to me! It seems like before we were married his whole life was a lie!" Sandra's beautifully expressive face was still swollen and bruised from the beating she had received several days earlier. "For two years we lived together and he never got mad. He was so laid back, nothing got to him. I loved that about him. These last few months he's been like an animal. I can't believe he had me fooled for so long." Sandra gazed out the window, lost in some other world for a moment. Then, with exhausted frustration she sighed, "I always swore this would never happen to me."

Sandra and Paul had been in love. At least it had sure looked that way. They spent a great deal of time together and were sexually involved almost immediately. They knew they wanted to get married but they were scared. Both had been deeply hurt in previous relationships. They decided that before taking the risk of marriage, and since they were having intercourse anyway, they would try living together for a while, just to see how it would work out.

For two years they had a positive experience together. They felt as though they communicated well and they seemed to resolve their occasional squabbles. Then they got married. After eight months their relationship was a complete disaster. To make the situation even more complex, Sandra was three months pregnant. Whatever resolution was going to take place for them, it would mean restructuring their relationship from the ground up. It would require lots of prayer, forgiveness, and hard work. Some couples can do it, though it's never easy. In Sandra and Paul's case, neither was willing to take the risk. The marriage ended in divorce.

THE DECEPTION OF COHABITATION

Cohabitation is the situation of an unmarried couple living together, presumably to test their compatibility before making a marriage commitment. Cohabitation is a trap all its own.

Many couples who have cohabited come to my office, usually some time after marriage. There is very little difference between their struggles and the struggles of couples who have never lived together. If anything, couples who have cohabited have more severe problems in certain areas than partners who have never "tested" marriage. The belief that cohabitation is a type of marriage is a serious misconception.

A recent newsletter of the Rockford Institute Center on The Family in America published these findings:

> 35 percent [of those who have cohabited] can be expected to have terminated their first marriage before 15 years, compared with only 19 percent among those who did not cohabit before marriage.

The authors of the study conjecture that

> those who do not have strong feelings against
> cohabiting before marriage may also find it easier
> to terminate a marriage that has gone sour.[3]

The key ingredient that differentiates living together from marriage is the "back door"—the option to leave without a lot of messy consequences. The logic goes something like this: "If things don't work out, we can chalk it up to experience and move on. At least we will have learned something about ourselves and marriage." This sounds good in theory, but it doesn't work out that way in real life. There are several reasons for that.

DOUBLE MESSAGES

When two opposite messages are communicated about the same situation at the same time, we call it a "double message." The classic double message is a parent saying to his teenager, "I want you to be independent, so do what I tell you!" or "I've told you a million times, never exaggerate!" That's pretty confusing to the kid.

Most people are aware that communication is more than just an exchange of words. We communicate far more intensely and clearly with our behavior than we do verbally. It has been estimated that nonverbal messages are five times as powerful as the spoken word. This means that if my words say one thing and my behavior says another, you'll tend to believe my behavior even if you don't want to. The old saying "Actions speak louder than words" is true.

Cohabiting couples communicate nonverbal double messages every day. Let's use Sandra and Paul as our example. They were deeply in love and wanted to be together constantly. They felt as though they were ready for marriage, but each had been surprised and hurt in previous relationships that had broken up. Both were strongly opposed to divorce since both came from broken homes. The most logical solution seemed to be for them to live together—for a few months, maybe a year or so, to check it out. What could be more reasonable? So they did just that.

By moving in together, Sandra and Paul were communicating a message to one another. That message was, "I desire intimacy with you. I want to get to know you deeply. I want to be one with you, and only living together will allow me to be that trusting and close to you." Picture them with arms open, coming toward each other.

But there's also a second message. It is conveyed by the fact that one or both of them were not willing to make the commitment of marriage. This message says, "Don't get too close, there's a limit. I don't want to get so close that I can't escape if you hurt me. I'm not sure I can trust you." The picture here is of Sandra and Paul, arms outstretched, backing away slowly.

Sandra and Paul may not have been consciously aware of the conflicting messages they were communicating to each other, but the messages came through loud and clear.

DEAD END

The result of the double message is an inbred lack of confidence in the relationship. What is real and what is not real become confused. What is said and what is believed become two different things. Distrust and doubt are integrated at the very core of the relationship.

After marriage these couples are surprised to discover how dissatisfied they have suddenly become. They feel an uneasiness that wasn't there before; it is beyond their understanding. What happened to this logical, well-planned relationship?

What happened is this: The wedding shut the back door. Their comfortable relationship began to close around them like a room with shrinking walls. This is exactly what they were trying to avoid! Suddenly their worst fears have come true. "Omigosh! What have I gotten myself into?" Since distrust and insecurity were built into the relationship long ago, the downhill slide to disaster isn't far away.

In a healthy marriage, commitment is at the very heart of the relationship, regardless of the ebb and flow of emotions. For Sandra and Paul, commitment was added on as a final touch.

MORE SURPRISES

There is another reason the theory of a "trial marriage" doesn't hold up. When a couple lives together without the commitment of marriage, the little irritations of daily living are no big deal:

> He doesn't clean out the bathtub, but so what? If you get tired of it you can leave, right? No reason to make a fuss.

> You're bothered by the way she blows her nose. No big deal. Since you're just testing this thing out, you focus on "real" problems.

Besides, if you can just let it slide, go to bed and make love, everything will be fine in the morning. And so it goes, in a hundred ways, most of which the individuals are not consciously aware of.

Then it happens. They close the back door with a marriage license. The impact of those little irritations seems to change, each one setting a lifetime precedent. The emotional response is, "It's going to be like this forever! It has to change, now!" Those previously "unnoticed" little irritations are hair triggers for frequent conflict, and it's a real surprise to both partners since neither seemed to mind them before! Now each person starts believing that he or she has been deceived, betrayed, and trapped.

What happened to the trial marriage? *There is no such thing.* Trying to experience marriage without a lifetime commitment is like going to a doughnut shop to buy your meals. You can fill your stomach and convince yourself that you've taken nourishment, but eventually you'll die of malnutrition with your stomach full.

Is It Too Late for Us?

What about the married couple who began their union by living together before marriage and are now experiencing disillusionment? Is there hope for them? Yes, there is. But subtle relational patterns and habits don't change easily. The following suggestions, if conscientiously applied, can help restructure negative patterns.

1. Realize that the habit of emotional guardedness and distrust has been a subtle part of the relationship from the beginning. It's important to recognize that this pattern has complicated normal marital conflicts with misunderstanding and overreaction.

2. Commit yourself before God to work through the complications created by your early relationship. This is not a demand you make on your spouse, it is a decision you make for yourself.

3. Educate yourself about healthy marital communication patterns. Books and cassette tapes on marriage by authors such as H. Norman Wright, James Dobson, and Gary Smalley will be very helpful. These will help you differentiate between what is normal, healthy, and productive and what is defensive, reactive, and destruc-

tive. They will also help you develop new and more effective patterns of communication and conflict resolution in your marriage.

4. Consciously work on straightening out the double messages regarding commitment to your relationship. Do this with regular affirmation of your trust in and love for one another. This is especially important during times of conflict and dissatisfaction. Remind your partner that you are committed to the relationship, even when the relationship isn't particularly enjoyable.

5. If there are conflicts and negative feelings which cannot be resolved by the two of you, don't hesitate to find a professionally trained Christian marriage counselor to help you work through these issues.

Premarital relationships headed for destruction can be saved if the couple truly desires to redirect their focus towards developing emotional and spiritual closeness. Let me tell you about one couple who successfully redirected their relationship.

Retraced Steps

I had known Nate and Carol for several years. I met them through my work with Christian singles ministries. They were one of several couples who became acquainted at a conference where I spoke, and we had run into each other occasionally as their relationship developed. Now they had come to see me for premarital counseling. I was delighted to hear they were planning to be married.

Both Nate and Carol were fairly new Christians when they met. Both of them had grown considerably during their several years of courtship. They were a sharp, sincere, excited Christian couple. However, they were sexually involved to the point of intercourse and felt guilty about it. A Christian friend had told them they were married in God's eyes so it was all right to have sex. That confused them but it seemed to make sense. They told me that the main goal in coming for premarital counseling was to improve communication and to enhance their emotional intimacy in preparation for marriage.

In our first session we discussed the fact that nowhere in the Bible is there an indication that a couple can be married "in God's eyes" and still be single. "In God's eyes" is a neat little phrase used to rationalize all kinds of questionable behavior. It has nothing to do with the reality of Scripture.

> *For you know what commandments we gave you by the authority of the Lord Jesus. For this is the will of God, your sanctification; that is that you abstain from sexual immorality; that each of you know how to possess his own vessel in sanctification and honor, not in lustful passion, like the Gentiles who do not know God; and that no man transgress and defraud his brother in the matter because the Lord is the avenger in all these things, just as we also told you before and solemnly warned you. For God has not called us for the purpose of impurity, but in sanctification. Consequently, he who rejects this is not rejecting man but the God who gives His Holy Spirit to you* (1 Thessalonians 4:2-8, NASB).

I pointed out that although their sexual behavior was clearly condemned in Scripture, there was forgiveness and healing at the Cross through repentance, as with any sin. Now it was imperative they recognize the need to redirect the focus of their relationship to the development of *genuine* intimacy. Through subsequent counseling sessions they came to understand that the hallmark of genuine intimacy is communication, and that even though they were committed to becoming married, continuing their sexual relationship would eventually stunt their capacity to truly know one another.

ARTIFICIAL INTIMACY

The need for emotional closeness and intimacy is inherent in human nature. Everyone wants to be loved for who they are, not just for what they can do or give to someone else. The sexual bond is intended to be an expression of that intimacy, but it can never be the source of it. This is a distinction that many people fail to make.

In our society we have been taught to label sex "intimate." In fact, the words *sex* and *intimacy* are often used interchangeably. This reflects a gross misunderstanding of the true nature of intimacy. It also propagates a myth about the role of sex in relationships.

Webster's dictionary defines intimacy as "a familiarity characterizing one's deepest nature, a close association marked by warm friendship developing through long association." It is knowing and being known—deeply. That takes time and effort, lots of it.

A couple's sexual relationship prior to marriage can easily create what I call "artificial intimacy." There is a sensation of closeness inherent in mutual sexual arousal. Yet that sensation is deceptive because it can feel intimate when it is not. To be intimate with another person is to be vulnerable, emotionally open, and trusting. Think about that for a moment. *Sexual intercourse can occur without any of that being true.* If sex were truly and necessarily intimate, prostitution couldn't exist! However, it is physically possible to have a sexual relationship with a complete stranger and still have that false sense of intimacy. A couple may feel close when they are not close at all.

THE ALL-PURPOSE PROBLEM SOLVER?

Sex can even be used to *avoid* intimacy. Couples do it all the time, most of them without knowing it. Here's how it works. When emotional needs are not being met or when some problem exists, tension and conflict thrive.

The tension may result from a disagreement or from a difference in perspective, values, or mood. For example, he may live from paycheck to paycheck, while she learned to save and budget money at an early age. Or she may want to spend what he thinks is an inordinate amount of time with her parents; after all, he was on his own from the age of sixteen. Whatever the source of the conflict, it almost always means that something needs to be talked out. It can be a sign of life and health in a relationship. But when conflict isn't resolved, it becomes a barrier to closeness. When conflict is ignored, hidden, or denied, the relationship is in danger.

Sexually active couples often use the *sensation* of intimacy to deny the existence of conflict. A couple can go to bed, feel great about each other, and never resolve the real issue. Problems don't get resolved, they just get buried under artificial intimacy.

This pattern can continue for a long time. In fact, it often remains hidden until unresolved tension develops into resentment. Frequently, the woman feels this first. As resentment builds, sexual intercourse no longer feels intimate because the emotional barriers are so high. This usually happens after a couple has been married for a while. Then the response is usually one of hopelessness. He or she may say things like, "All the love has gone out of our marriage; there's nothing left." The issue isn't that something has gone out of the relationship but that something was built into it—a pattern of escape and denial based on sexual feelings of arousal instead of healthy communication.

To help Nate and Carol understand this concept I shared the following illustration. A couple's relationship before marriage can be compared to a steam pipe that contains and transports pressure. The pipe has several small cracks invisible to the eye. At one end of the pipe is an exhaust valve which can be opened or closed. As long as the valve is open, the pressure is released and the cracks never emit any steam—they are never discovered and repaired. Eventually they will corrode and destroy the pipe. The valve must be *closed* so that pressure can build; then the cracks can be discovered and repaired.

All couples have weak points in their communication patterns: different viewpoints, biases, sensitivities, family differences, role expectations. All of us have them. Since communication is the area of real intimacy, these "cracks" are important to discover. But if a couple is opening the exhaust valve of sex, normal pressure doesn't have the chance to build. Many communication "flaws" won't become evident until they are severe. And for many couples, that is too late.

What Nate and Carol came to understand is this: By continuing their sexual relationship, they were keeping the valve open. As long as they were releasing pressure that way, they could not accomplish their premarital counseling objectives. They needed to close the valve to realistically evaluate their patterns of communication. As they stopped releasing emotional pressure sexually, they began to experience irritations and reactions that hadn't been evident. The "cracks" emitted some "steam," and they began to discover what to work on in their relationship in preparation for marriage.

Nate and Carol found a powerful side benefit. Since they had to find new ways of dealing with their sexual feelings, they learned to be creative in expressing affection. Written notes, small but significant gifts, shared secrets, shared feelings (both positive and negative) in serious conversation all became new ways of expressing affection toward one another. Nate and Carol learned many lessons in the art of romance that would pay rich dividends in their future marriage.

If they had kept the sexual valve open, premarital counseling would have been a waste of time and money, and they would have set themselves up for potential marital problems later on. Fortunately, Nate and Carol understood the seriousness of their situation and were willing to do whatever it took to prepare for marriage. Some of the steps I suggested to them will be discussed in a later chapter on setting standards in dating and courtship.

GROWING CLOSER

1) What is your definition of intimacy? Is it different from the definition in this chapter?

2) Is there something about you that you are unwilling to share with someone else . . . such as a fear, a failure, or some deep hurt from your past?

Write down the characteristics of a relationship in which you would feel safe sharing this fact with another person. Be as specific as you can.

What does this list of characteristics tell you about your concept of intimacy?

3) Think of the person you would call your closest friend, or if you are married, think of your spouse. Would you say that you are emotionally intimate with him or her?

What behaviors are you using to define intimacy in this relationship?

4) Think of a friend with whom you are not emotionally intimate. What are the differences between that relationship and the one mentioned in question 2?

For those who are married:

First, as individuals and *without sharing your answers with your partner,* write down your responses to the following statements as honestly and completely as you can.

---

1) Circle your opinion in the appropriate column:

1	2	3	4	5
strongly agree	mildly agree	undecided	mildly disagree	strongly disagree

Husband   Wife

1 2 3 4 5 Our relationship is as emotionally   1 2 3 4 5
intimate as I would like it to be

1 2 3 4 5 I openly share my thoughts and   1 2 3 4 5
feelings without reservation

1 2 3 4 5 My spouse openly shares thoughts   1 2 3 4 5
and feelings without reservation

1 2 3 4 5 During courtship we were more   1 2 3 4 5
emotionally intimate than we
are now

2) Now go back and predict what you believe your spouse's responses will be. Use the other column for these answers.

3) Circle the appropriate response:

When I begin to feel emotionally vulnerable, my reaction is to . . .

open up and share   become irritable and
  my fears   angry
withdraw in silence   crack a joke
change the subject   act as if it doesn't
make sexual advances   matter

4) From the above list, my partner's response to emotional vulnerability usually is _____ .

5) One thing I could do to deepen emotional intimacy in my marriage is _____ .

6) One thing I think my partner could do to deepen our emotional intimacy is _____ .

Now, set aside an hour or two as a couple and discuss your individual responses.

The couple who are sexually active prior to marriage are conditioning themselves to respond to a fetish. It can be, and often is, devastating to sexual enjoyment after marriage.

3

THE ILLICITNESS TRAP

R emember Pavlov from your high school psychology days? He trained a dog to salivate in response to the ringing of a bell. It was a physiological response stimulated by something not naturally associated with the response.

In the same way, even without realizing it, we can teach our bodies to react in ways they wouldn't normally! We call that teaching process "conditioning."

With this in mind, we need to realize that our response of sexual arousal can be conditioned very quickly, perhaps more readily than any other physiological response. The term *arousal* refers to the physical experience of excitement that surrounds the sexual experience, such as increased heart rate, increased blood pressure, tension, erection in males, lubrication in females. All of these are part of that physiological arousal process.

An individual's repeated exposure to sexually stimulating material—pictures, books, films, objects, and

41

countless other things—will affect or condition his or her sexual response. Arousal then becomes dependent on what is known as a fetish—sexual excitement requiring a non-living object as the focus of that arousal.

Randy's story outlines a very sad but common illustration of this trap. Randy had grown up in a conservative Christian home with high moral values, but he became heavily involved in pornography prior to his marriage to Louise. Louise was an attractive woman in her early twenties who, like Randy, had come from a Christian home environment.

Randy had assumed that his desire for pornography would disappear when he and Louise were married. To Randy's dismay, he often had trouble becoming aroused by his new bride. More and more he found himself desiring, and even needing, to be exposed to some sort of pornography in order to function sexually with her. At first he tried to hide his literature, but after several embarrassing experiences of being discovered he gave up trying. Eventually he began subscribing to the Playboy channel on their cable TV, though he would never watch it when Louise was around. Feeling increasingly guilty about his "habit," Randy soon stopped attending church with Louise as dissatisfaction in their relationship intensified.

Randy had developed a fetish for pornography without knowing it and certainly without intending to. For Randy the therapeutic process was a slow and emotionally painful one. Randy had to examine his deep feelings of inadequacy and fears of rejection. He also had to face his pattern of escaping into fantasy with imaginary sex partners, which made him dissatisfied with reality. These problems had developed over a period of years and would not change quickly. Faith, determination, honesty, forgiveness, and a mutual commitment by both Randy and

Louise turned a very painful experience into regrettable history.

THE FETISH OF ILLICITNESS

It may be surprising to know that participation in premarital sex creates a fetish very similar to Randy's experience. The couple who are sexually active prior to marriage are conditioning themselves to respond to a fetish. The process is subtle. It can be, and often is, devastating to sexual enjoyment after marriage.

There is within each of us, especially those of us raised in a Judeo-Christian value system, an awareness that premarital sex is wrong. It may be deeply buried, repressed, ignored, or openly defied, but it's there. If we allow ourselves to listen to our feelings carefully and long enough, we will hear it. Something deep within us says, "We shouldn't be doing this . . . ," and there is something exciting about that! There is definitely a stimulating quality in that "wrongness." The term I use to describe this experience is *illicitness*.

Often our awareness of illicitness gets translated into self-talk—statements we make to ourselves—such as:

"What if someone finds out?"
"I'll show my folks I can do what I want!"
"See how much we love each other?"
"No out-dated church is going to control me!"

I've talked with countless married couples, Christian and non-Christian alike, who have said to me: "Roger, before we were married we had a great sex life! It was exciting, fulfilling, enjoyable. But, for some reason, on our wedding night that excitement died. It has never been very good since."

43

What do you suppose happened to those couples on their wedding night? What happened was that the illicitness, which had become a conditioned (required) sexual stimulus, was taken away! Who would be offended or impressed by their behavior now? They were no longer "proving" something with their sexual relationship. In fact, sex was now mandatory for them since a well-adjusted marriage includes sexual interaction on a regular basis.

How does a person who has experienced the excitement of illicitness usually try to recapture it after he or she is married? One very simple method is to have an affair . . . bingo! Good sex again. Since there is also an awareness within each of us that extramarital sex is wrong, illicitness is a part of any adulterous relationship. The result? Marriages crumble, families are torn apart, and the divorce rate climbs.

God seldom seems to spend much time explaining why He gives us certain instructions. As our Creator, He takes the liberty of telling us what will make us operate to our maximum potential, and He expects us to pay attention. When we ignore His warnings we risk losing that potential, and we settle for a situation that is less fulfilling than it could have been.

Lost Potential?

Let's explore the effects of the illicitness trap further. The better our understanding, the better equipped we will be to avoid the trap as well as to help others avoid it.

Sexual enjoyment and responsiveness are always maximized by the absence of external tension. In other words, stress of any kind detracts from sexual fulfillment. Relaxation, contentment, and trust in both the environment and the relationship are extremely important variables for pleasure and enjoyment in the sexual experience.

There are a number of factors in most premarital sexual relationships which intensify stress and minimize sexual fulfillment for both male and female:

1. *The premarital sexual relationship fosters guilt and anxiety in both partners. The lack of a tangible, permanent commitment results in a certain level of insecurity.*

Beyond the sense of illicitness discussed earlier, there is fear of rejection. Since the relationship does not have the foundation of a lifetime commitment, each partner is likely to think, *He or she may not like how I am or what I do* or *I may not be good enough.* This results in a preoccupation with one's own performance and a fear of failure. Whenever a person cannot abandon himself completely to his partner in trust, confidence, and security, sexual satisfaction is minimized. This insecurity is often more intense for the woman. According to Dr. Helen Singer Kaplan, noted authority on sexual therapy:

> A trusting, loving relationship is important to insure sexual functioning. For a woman, a feeling of trust that the partner will meet her needs, particularly the dependency needs, and a feeling of security that the spouse will take care of her, will take responsibility for her, will not abandon her and will be loyal to her seem necessary in order to enable her to abandon herself to sexual pleasures. In fact, recent evidence indicates that trust may be one of the most important factors determining orgasmic capacity in women.[4]

2. *Premarital sex is often hurried.*

Usually, the time or place is less than convenient to avoid detection. The need for gentle, patient stimulation as well as communication and expressions of love is neglected or altogether ignored. The caring part of the relationship tends to be set aside and the focus becomes personal physical satisfaction.

3. *The goal of the male involved is usually physical release rather than sharing or meeting his partner's needs.*

Since female arousal is generally more gradual than that of a male's, the focus is on his satisfaction. Many times she feels used or neglected.

4. *The premarital sexual experience is generally approached with little or no contraceptive preparation.*

The possibility of pregnancy brings with it a tension of its own.

5. *Increased numbers of young people are facing the prospect of sexually transmitted diseases.*

All of these factors support the conclusion that premarital sex is *never* sex at its best. When a couple has forfeited the chance to experience sex within the secure relationship of a marriage commitment, they don't understand what they have given up! Unfortunately, they may never be able to experience sex at its best. They may never know what they could have experienced together had they been obedient to the warnings of Scripture.

For the couple who may now be thinking they should break up because their relationship is doomed, let me shine a ray of light. I know from my counseling experience that it is possible for an unmarried couple who has been sexually active to recapture that potential, at least to some degree. However, it doesn't happen by accident; it is accomplished through conscious decisions and commitment. *It means ending all sexual intercourse and setting some clear limits on the physical relationship for a period of time prior to the wedding* (the longer the better). Together the couple must make some serious decisions about how to handle their natural sexual temptations so that appropriate patterns can be established. In chapter 9 we will discuss how a couple goes about restructuring their physical relationship.

For the married couple who recognizes and understands these patterns—and the consequences to their marriage—there are several steps that will help begin the process of positive change. Some of the issues you will need to discuss together may feel awkward or threatening at first; it is important to discuss them despite this feeling. Relationship growth seldom occurs in a marriage without communication.

1. Set aside some time to be alone as a couple and discuss your early sexual patterns. Share what you would like to have changed in your courtship. Be sure to think about and explain why these changes would have been important. At the end of this chapter is a section designed to help begin the conversation.

2. Confess to one another and to God the mistakes you made in courtship. Discuss your understanding of the impact of those mistakes on your current relationship.

3. Make a decision to forgive both your partner and yourself for the past. Forgiveness means no longer requiring payment for the wrongs committed against you. In relationships these "payments" can take many forms: withdrawal, silence, angry outbursts, brooding resentment, lack of cooperation. Forgiveness may not miraculously change the relationship, but without forgiveness there can be no real change.

4. Learn to discuss your sexual relationship openly with one another. What are your desires, preferences, dreams, fears? This may not be a single conversation but many conversations over a long period of time.

5. Read and discuss the following books:

Re-Bonding by Dr. Donald Joy
Intended for Pleasure by Dr. Ed Wheat

6) If both of you feel little progress toward the changes you desire after taking these steps, consider finding a Christian professional marriage counselor or therapist. Your pastor may be helpful in locating one.

GROWING CLOSER

Draw a line from the physical level on the left to what you believe to be the appropriate commitment level on the right.

PHYSICAL LEVEL	COMMITMENT LEVEL
Holding Hands	Casual Relationship
Hugging	
Kissing	First Date
French Kissing	
Caressing, above the neck	Steady Dating
Caressing, below the neck	
Petting, (underneath clothing, no sexual organs)	Exclusive Dating
Petting, (underneath clothing, sexual organs)	Engagement
Sexual Intercourse	Marriage

1)   How do your beliefs expressed in this exercise actually apply to your relationships?

2)   If you are dating or are engaged, how does your opinion on the above exercise compare to your partner's opinion? (Try having him/her do the same exercise before you share your responses. You may learn a lot about how well you know each other.)

3)   How do differences in this area affect a courtship relationship?

For those who are married:

Take some time to complete the following statements as honestly and thoroughly as you can. After completing them individually, share your responses and discuss your feelings about them.

1) If I could change one thing from our courtship, it would be _____.

2) The reason I would have made this change is ____
_____.

3) A change I can make in this area *now* is _____
_____.

4) The thing I most appreciate about our sexual relationship is _____.

5) For me, the most helpful change in our sexual relationship would be _____.

Some things I can do to facilitate this change are ____
_____ . Something I think you could do to help this change is _____ .

Couples in the petting stage generally don't talk much, at least not in depth.

4

THE TECHNICAL VIRGINITY TRAP

A few years ago I was addressing a youth leadership conference on the topic of sexuality for Christians. Following one of the workshops a young woman asked a very pertinent question. I remember the situation specifically because every single person present leaned forward and nodded their approval of the question. I had obviously left out something very important in my talk.

"I've recently gotten engaged. My fiancé and I have worked hard to keep our relationship sexually pure. But we have strong feelings for each other, and we are very affectionate. After hearing what you've said today, something confuses me. Can petting be damaging to a relationship, or are we just talking about sleeping together?"

Her question was a good one and deserved a direct answer. However, the answer is more complex than just yes or no. I hope I was able to give her an adequate answer in the short time we had that day. This chapter will answer that same sticky question as thoroughly as possible.

Petting is a difficult term to define clearly. Certainly, petting involves two individuals touching one another in some sensual manner, but that may be the only similarity in many definitions. Some definitions revolve around which specific parts of the body are caressed by another person. Many definitions will describe petting in terms of two levels: "light petting," which usually means the couple is clothed, and "heavy petting," which usually means the couple is undressed. For our purposes, petting is mutual sexual stimulation without sexual intercourse, or coitus, as its goal. It involves building sexual tension through fondling another person's sexually excitable areas without relieving that tension through intercourse. Petting may or may not involve orgasm.

If we think of sexual behavior on a continuum from holding hands to coitus, petting could be described as more intense than a kiss and hug, but less intense than intercourse. Of course, because of the arousal of sexual desire, many couples who intend to go no further than petting will end up having intercourse. When a couple intends to have intercourse, this type of fondling is called "foreplay." So in this sense, the only difference between petting and foreplay is one of intention.

Some people think petting is a way for two people who care for one another and value their virginity to give each other sexual pleasure without going "all the way." They think it is a way for two people who are committed to each other, though unmarried, to begin emotional preparation for a sexual relationship without violating the biblical code of sexual abstinence. Others recognize that petting is a type of defrauding because it arouses desires and fantasies which morally cannot be fulfilled. They realize that however much the individuals care for each other, they are creating a bond meant only for marriage . . . without any guarantee they will remain together.

THE PROGRESSION

There is a natural progression in sexual stimulation and arousal. It develops from something as subtle as a smile to something as powerful as intercourse. It includes holding hands, kissing, caressing, fondling, and many stages in-between. The common denominator in all these behaviors is the direction. That direction is to intensify, increase, and progress.

It's a fact that each stage becomes less and less satisfying with time. Once you progress from hand-holding to kissing, it is extremely difficult to return to only hand-holding without a feeling of dissatisfaction. Our physiological sensations urge us toward intercourse. That's not a bad thing necessarily; within the commitment of marriage it is an incredibly exciting and emotionally strengthening bond. Outside of that commitment it can be a lot like quicksand.

Emotional intimacy emerges through identifiable stages of contact. Each of these stages is an essential component in the development toward the "emotional covenant" of becoming husband and wife. This sense of oneness is what gives a healthy marriage relationship its almost mystical uniqueness among all other relationships. These stages nurture a special bond of companionship that draws two people together as no other relationship can. In his book *Intimate Behaviour*, well-known British zoologist/anthropologist Desmond Morris has described, in depth, the patterns of human intimacy. I have paraphrased and abridged his findings on courtship patterns.

1. Eye to body. A glance reveals so much about a person— sex, size, shape, age, personality, and status. The importance people place on these criteria determines whether or not they will be attracted to each other.

2. *Eye to Eye.* When the man and woman who are strangers to each other exchange glances, their most natural reaction is to look away, usually with embarrassment. If their eyes meet again, they may smile, which signals that they may like to become better acquainted.

3. *Voice to Voice.* Their initial conversations are trivial and include questions like "What is your name?" or "What do you do for a living?" During this long stage the two people learn much about each other's opinions, pastimes, activities, habits, hobbies, likes and dislikes. If they're compatible, they become friends.

4. *Hand to Hand.* The first instance of physical contact between the couple is usually a nonromantic occasion such as when the man helps the woman descend a high step or aids her across an obstacle. At this point either of the individuals can withdraw from the relationship without rejecting the other. However, if continued, hand-to-hand contact will eventually become an evidence of the couple's romantic attachment to each other.

5. *Hand to shoulder.* This affectionate embrace is still noncommittal. It is a "buddy" type position in which the man and woman are side by side. They are more concerned with the world in front of them than they are with each other. The hand-to-shoulder contact reveals a relationship that is more than a close friendship, but probably not real love.

6. *Arm to Waist.* Because this is something two people of the same sex would not ordinarily do, it is clearly romantic. They are close enough to be sharing secrets or intimate language with each other. Yet, as they walk side by side with hand to waist, they are still facing forward.

7. *Face to Face.* This level of contact involves gazing into one another's eyes, hugging and kissing. If none of the previous stages were skipped, the man and woman will have developed a special code from experience that enables them to engage communication with very few words. At this point sexual desire becomes an important factor in the relationship.

8. *Hand to Head.* This is an extension of the previous stage. The man and woman tend to cradle or stroke each other's head while kissing or talking. Rarely do individuals in our culture touch the head of another person unless they are either romantically involved or are family members. It is a designation of emotional closeness.

9-12. *The final steps.* The last four levels of involvement are distinctly sexual and private. They are (9) hand to body, (10) mouth to breast, (11) touching below the waist, and (12) intercourse.[5]

It is impossible to emphasize enough the importance of moving through each of these stages slowly and systematically. True intimacy between a man and woman grows gradually and gently. Time and patience are essential—the two aspects of courtship that cannot be rushed. When a couple moves too quickly or skips a stage, the natural emotional bonding process is disrupted and something is lost in the development of the emotional partnership between them.

As these twelve stages illustrate, the progression is toward genital-to-genital bonding, or intercourse. The behaviors we label "petting" involve steps nine through eleven. They are preliminary to intercourse and leave no room for further progression except intercourse. A couple who wants to avoid intercourse before marriage, who does not feel ready for a marriage commitment, and yet are involved in petting, have few options open besides failure or frustration. They are attempting to pursue and intensify a natural progression, only to abort it just prior to fulfillment.

This natural progression is the force that pushes a couple who have had intercourse to continue having it— even if they feel guilty about it. This progression is also what compels a person who has had intercourse in one relationship to pursue it in the next, even when he or she knows it was a problem in the first relationship.

For most couples, petting is like shifting a car into high gear—it generally speeds up the progression towards coitus. The pursuit of physical pleasure dominates the relationship, and emotional growth and communication often come to a screeching halt.

Couples who are in the petting stage generally don't talk much, at least not in depth. They neglect the exploration of each other's personalities in favor of exploring physical sensations. While the physical aspect escalates, the relationship stagnates. They give more and more attention and energy to being alone together and to satisfying their physical appetites. They spend less and less time being social with other people or with each other. The date becomes a time to "get through" in order to arrive at the real agenda for the evening—physical stimulation and arousal.

Before long there is very little left in the relationship besides physical involvement. Feeling close is dependent on physical contact, and giving it up feels like giving up the relationship. Sexual compulsion is almost inevitable. If a couple isn't willing to risk the loss of the relationship by backing away from physical intimacy, or if they just don't give it much thought, sex dominates the relationship even without intercourse.

Often the person who will have the most difficult time controlling this progression is the one with a deep need to be loved. This is a person who feels unloved, perhaps unlovable, and may be afraid, on a deep level, that he or she doesn't have anything to contribute to a relationship. The person who is searching to fill a void left by an affection-starved past is extremely susceptible to misreading relationship signals and often translates another person's selfish lust into a message of genuine love.

While the potential for this type of vulnerability is always there, most people would agree that physical involvement is a pitifully poor substitute for genuine love and caring.

Tim Stafford, who regularly provides a practical, biblical perspective on love and sex in a question-and-answer column for *Campus Life* magazine, puts it this way:

> In our culture, couples who have been going together for a while are likely to hug, kiss and hold hands. I think these are, for most people, warm and innocent ways to express loving appreciation. When you go further and aim for sexual excitement, I think you generally stop speaking the language of love. Why? Because you have to stop somewhere short of intercourse. Some people can't—they lose control. Some people lose the desire to stop. Some people keep control, but they do so at the cost of feeling frustrated. Instead of feeling warm toward

> each other, they feel overheated. I have never known
> this to help a relationship to grow, especially when
> people spend hours together revving up their
> motors and pushing the brakes at the same time.
> You'd be a lot better off just talking and getting to
> know each other.[6]

In Chapter 3 we discussed the trap of illicitness. This is the process of conditioning an individual's sexual response to inappropriate stimulus. We can't discuss the dangers involved in petting without dealing with illicitness, because the same principles apply. Any time sexual arousal is pursued for its own sake, as is generally the case with petting, the potential for problematic conditioning exists. If it's been awhile since you read the chapter on illicitness, you may want to go back and refresh your memory on the main points of the conditioning process before completing this chapter.

If petting is used to bolster a person's poor self-esteem, then self-esteem will soon come to depend on petting. If petting is used to feel close to another person, it will be difficult to feel close without petting. We just can't separate the phenomenon of conditioning from sexual arousal. We can only structure our sexual relationships so that we are conditioning appropriate arousal responses. We don't do that in just one or two experiences, we do it over the long haul. We do it by thoughtfully developing a relationship to be consistent with our values and goals.

THE BIBLICAL PERSPECTIVE

What does the Bible say about this area of sexual conduct?

It is commonly assumed that young people in biblical times reached puberty at a somewhat later age than they do today. The difference is usually attributed to the improved diet and medical care children have today. Whatever the reason, the average age of this sexual transition was probably about fourteen or fifteen. Marriage probably occurred at about the same age, so there was not much need to deal with sexual tension outside of marriage. Contact between the sexes was also limited. Generally boys attended school while girls didn't, and marriages were arranged by parents. Also, a young person's sexual contact was closely guarded by the parents because a daughter's virginity strongly affected her father's dowry or "bride price." Dad had financial reasons to protect his daughter's sex life before marriage.

Circumstances are different for young people today. From the time they are very young, boys and girls are usually not segregated. They spend a great deal of time together. The average age of puberty is younger today, usually twelve or thirteen. The average age of marriage in the U.S. is much older, twenty-three to twenty-five. This gives young people a period of sexual maturity and sexual tension that rarely existed two thousand years ago. It also creates many opportunities to experiment with sexual relationships—rare in biblical times.

Physical desire and contact naturally increase as a couple moves closer to a marriage commitment. As sexual passion builds, perspective is distorted—good intentions are often lost in the rush of emotions and physical sensations. Motives can quickly change from benevolence to self-gratification, from affection to lust. And when your goal becomes sexual excitement instead of an appropriate expression of love and commitment, you have entered a danger zone that often means the destruction of a healthy, growing relationship.

Does the Bible say petting is right or wrong? While there are clear passages regarding sexual intercourse outside of marriage, other sexual behaviors such as petting aren't discussed directly. But we can clearly discern God's viewpoint from passages that deal with lust and self-discipline.

> *"You have heard that it was said, 'Do not commit adultery.' But I tell you that anyone who looks at a woman lustfully has already committed adultery with her in his heart"* (Matthew 5:27-28).

Jesus is pointing out that sins can be committed "in the heart" even if outward behavior doesn't carry out that sin.

> *"Now to the unmarried and the widows I say: It is good for them to stay unmarried, as I am. But if they cannot control themselves, they should marry, for it is better to marry than to burn with passion"* (1 Corinthians 7:8-9).

> *"Flee from youthful lusts, and pursue righteousness, faith, love and peace, with those who call on the Lord from a pure heart"* (2 Timothy 2:22, NASB).

> *"Flee from sexual immorality. All other sins a man commits are outside his body, but he who sins sexually sins against his own body. Do you not know that your body is a temple of the Holy Spirit, who is in you, whom you have received from God? You are not your own; you were bought at a price. Therefore honor God with your body"* (1 Corinthians 6:18-20).

The message is clear—it is a warning sign with flashing lights and blaring siren. God is telling us to run as fast as we can from sexual impurity. He is saying there is extreme danger in fostering sexual thoughts and intentions outside of a marriage relationship.

How, then, should a single person handle sexual desire? How can a person take the guesswork out of right and wrong sexual behavior? This author says it well.

> From Jesus' viewpoint, all of life should be governed by a deep love for God and other people. Instead of determining what to do in each of our many daily decisions by reflecting upon what is required by some law, Jesus would ask, "What is the most ethical and loving thing I could do in this situation?" His focus was upon what is right, not upon what is legal. The question for him was not "What can I get away with in order to gratify my own desires?" but "How can I best serve God and give of myself to help others?"
>
> Life lived on the level of manipulation is in actuality subhuman, a cheap imitation of real life. The idea of two people *using* each other to satisfy their physical appetites would be repugnant to Jesus and the Apostle Paul. They would assert that selfish living is truncated living, that pleasure gained through using others is only a pitiful shadow of the real joy involved in giving yourself unselfishly for another and happily receiving back what that person gives to you. This is not at all to diminish sexual desire or pleasure but to put them in their rightful place. Sex should be an enjoyable part of married life. . . . [7]

For an unmarried couple, there is another option besides breaking up or allowing sexual compulsion to dominate. That option is *starting over*. It means going back and resetting priorities and goals and deciding how to grow through the stages of physical involvement listed on pages 53-55, reserving the intimacies of steps 9-12 for marriage. Starting over is a difficult process. It takes a lot of commitment, and many relationships don't survive the tension. But if the goal of the relationship is marriage, it's well worth the effort. The fact is, if the relationship can't survive this kind of restructuring of priorities and behavior, it certainly won't survive the rigors of fifty years of life together!

PETTING WITHOUT A PARTNER

Another area of technical virginity, one of the most uncomfortable topics I can think of for most groups to discuss, is the topic of sexual self-stimulation, or masturbation. It is a topic loaded with guilt and fear. It's amazing, though, that any time I speak to a group of young people and ask them to write down anonymous questions for me, I can guarantee masturbation will come up many times. It's a big question on the minds of most single people.

In the past, masturbation has been blamed for everything from homosexuality to insanity, from laziness to hairy knuckles. Considering the way this question has been answered in past generations, it's not surprising that most people are uncomfortable even mentioning the word.

Masturbation is defined as manipulating one's own body in such a way as to arouse sexual tension. It is having sex without a partner and may or may not include orgasm. The physical sensation of arousal and release can occur with no relationship to another person.

SCRIPTURAL SILENCE

As in the case of petting, the Bible does not specifically mention masturbation. Genesis 38:8-10 is typically used as a passage teaching that God doesn't approve of masturbation. The biggest problem with using it for that reason is that masturbation wasn't involved! Onan had intercourse with his brother's widow as required by the Levirate law of inheritance; the situation was not one of self-stimulation. His problem was not a sexual one, but a direct violation of God's command.

The purpose of this particular law was to assure that the Hebrew lineage was carried on. It was a disaster when a man died without fathering children. To avoid this, the law commanded that the dead man's brother marry the widow and that children be raised as offspring of the deceased. The children would inherit his property and carry on his name (Deuteronomy 25:5-6).

Onan violated this law. He had intercourse with his brother's widow, but withdrew before orgasm and ejaculated onto the ground. He did this in order to avoid producing children for his brother. Onan was punished, not for masturbation but for violating God's law. So the one passage generally used as an example of masturbation in the Bible isn't an example of masturbation at all. The reason this passage is so often used is that there are no others. However, Scripture does specifically denounce lust and any behavior that would promote or reinforce impure thoughts.

DANGERS OF SELF-STIMULATION

For the teenager who has the sexual urges of adulthood but is in no way ready for a marriage commitment, self-stimulation for sexual release would appear to be a natural phase of sexual development that is left behind as meaningful relationships are developed with the opposite sex. For adults who, for various reasons, remain single, masturbation would appear to serve the same purpose. After all, it is sexual gratification without the complications of pregnancy, disease, or rejection.

But if it were this simple, there would be no struggle with the feelings of loneliness, emptiness, and guilt that are usually associated with masturbation. These are feelings that seem to describe most people's emotional responses to self-stimulation. The feelings of emptiness and isolation shouldn't surprise us when we consider God's purpose for sex—a relationship created as the expression of a lifelong bond between two committed and loving individuals. Masturbation then, is a replacement for a relationship. It is an inadequate substitute for sexual oneness with a life partner.

Although it's foolish to assume masturbation can satisfy one's need to be close to another person, neither should it be a source of self-hatred. There are many issues in life that are worth struggling over, such as our concept of God and our relationship to him, our forgiveness of others, and our concept of our own worth. We must not magnify the issue of masturbation out of proportion. A good measurement for an individual questioning the rightness or wrongness of masturbation is, Does it promote lust?

There are dangers involved in sexual self-stimulation, and we need to discuss some that may not be obvious on the surface. They relate to self-stimulation *as a habit.* They are problems both for the individual now, and for his or her future marriage relationship.

COMPULSIVITY

Let's consider the hypothetical case of John, a twenty-two-year-old single Christian man. John is rather unsure of himself socially. Though he is competent and successful as a computer programmer and is well accepted in his small circle of friends, he struggles with self-doubt and low self-esteem. As a result of these feelings, John tends to be shy and withdrawn in relationships and has never dated steadily. John compulsively masturbates to orgasm two to three times daily. He is deeply ashamed of his habit but feels powerless to stop.

In John's situation, as with many young people whom John represents, he has found a temporary escape from his negative emotions through sexual self-stimulation. In this pattern of escape, a cycle is established that leads to a literal addiction to masturbation. This cycle is illustrated below:

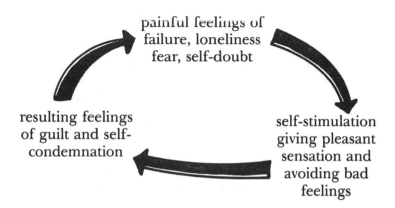

painful feelings of
failure, loneliness
fear, self-doubt

resulting feelings
of guilt and self-
condemnation

self-stimulation
giving pleasant
sensation and
avoiding bad
feelings

As the diagram illustrates, the compulsion begins with John's poor self-concept and his desire for an escape from negative feelings. The escape is temporary, of course, and results in deeper feelings of failure and self-doubt which increase his desire to escape into pleasant sensations.

Resolution for John will not lie in increased self-discipline—gritting his teeth and fighting the urge to masturbate, but in learning to view himself as an adequate person, worthy of being loved. Part of the solution will involve learning to establish appropriate, healthy relationships with women. He needs to let other people meet his emotional needs and to accept the risks of building relationships. As he does this, John will probably find his compulsion to masturbate lessening until this ineffective and inappropriate method of receiving nurturance is replaced by more satisfying relationships with other people.

POOR SEXUAL HABITS

Jim married Peggy when he was twenty-seven. Prior to his marriage he masturbated several times a week for sexual release. Jim didn't feel good about the practice, but it clearly wasn't an obsession with him. Since it wasn't affecting his life in any negative way, he didn't give it much thought. After their marriage, however, the newlyweds found themselves in a frustrating dilemma. It was clear that Jim had a serious problem with premature ejaculation. He found it extremely difficult to delay his ejaculation long enough for Peggy to be sexually satisfied. Frequently Jim would ejaculate during foreplay. The resulting frustration and embarrassment caused serious problems in their young marriage. Though he didn't realize it at the time, Jim's problem was the result of his earlier masturbation pattern.

A man and a woman generally do not reach orgasm at the same pace. It is a common struggle, especially with new husbands, to slow down their arousal process in order to allow their wives to reach a climax also. An individual who has masturbated consistently has developed some bad habits. The reason for this is that in self-stimulation there are no considerations other than one's own satisfaction. Since the purpose is sexual release, the goal in masturbation is usually to reach a climax as quickly as possible. This commonly results in a pattern of premature ejaculation after marriage.

Premature ejaculation is seldom considered a serious sexual dysfunction and is not difficult to treat in therapy. It can, however, be extremely frustrating to a couple and can be the source of other marital problems of miscommunication and resentment. Women who masturbate compulsively frequently experience inhibited sexual arousal. I should also mention that premarital sexual intercourse, because of its focus on self-satisfaction, often results in the same problem of premature ejaculation.

THE ACCELERATION PROBLEM

Another hazard of masturbation, inherent in almost all sexual activity, is the tendency to increase the behavior the more it is practiced. In other words, the more you do it, the more you want it. Masturbation doesn't function as a release of sexual pressure in the long run; actually, it is just the opposite. While an individual may experience some release of sexual pressure immediately following masturbation, sexual activity generally leads to increased sexual drive. So self-stimulation, as with other sexual activities such as intercourse or petting, tends to draw the individual toward more activity.

If the goal is to reduce pressure, it would be more helpful to concentrate on redirecting one's mental and emotional focus on some other interest. This means looking outward, developing relationships—male and female—that are healthy and close . . . but not sexual. It also means developing interests and hobbies that build self-esteem, self-satisfaction, and a feeling of success. Most importantly, it means avoiding exposure to sexually arousing material: pornographic literature, sexually suggestive television or movies, and other materials that cause heightened sexual desire. In our present culture it is probably unrealistic to think we could totally eliminate such input from our lives. However, a great deal can be avoided through a little effort. In the long run, all of these suggestions are more effective ways of reducing sexual pressure than masturbation.

Let me summarize what I've tried to say about the issue of masturbation.

- Don't be consumed with self-condemnation. While masturbation is far from the best expression of sexual bonding, it is not the "unforgivable" sin. It will not make you mentally ill, lazy, or homosexual.

67

- It will not resolve your feelings of loneliness, fear, or inadequacy; it is not a substitute for relational closeness.

- Indiscriminate practice of masturbation may develop some physical and mental habits that will need to be broken to enjoy a healthy marriage relationship.

- Masturbation is not a short-cut to anything; it is short-term sexual release without a partner.

Maintaining "technical" virginity, whether through petting or masturbation, is often destructive and never helpful to a developing relationship. Both behaviors promote confusion, frustration, and guilt, especially in those who want to follow the biblical standard of sexual purity.

If you had eight o'clock reservations at a four-star restaurant, would you go to a fast-food drive-in at seven o'clock? Most likely you wouldn't want to spoil your appetite; you would consider the enjoyment and ceremony of dinner at the fancy restaurant well worth the wait.

Similarly, God has given "four stars" to marriage, and He has designed us so that we can only be fulfilled within its exclusivity.

GROWING CLOSER

1	2	3	4	5	6	7	8	9	10

extremely   perfectly
uncomfortable   at peace

1) Place an "X" on the scale to indicate how comfortable you are, or have been in the past, with your physical relationships with the opposite sex.

2) Where do you think your partner would place his or her mark?

3) What specific changes would need to take place in order for you to place your mark on 10?

4) How would you go about making those changes?

It may be unrealistic to assume that something treated as taboo for years can be reversed 180 degrees on the wedding day.

5

THE ABSTINENCE TRAP

———————————————————————————

B ob and Jane had been married three weeks when they first came to see me. Jane was extremely depressed. Bob was frustrated. Both expressed disillusionment with their sexual relationship.

"When we were dating, we did everything right!" said Bob, almost angrily. "We prayed, we read the Bible, we talked a lot, we never had sex, we followed all the rules! In spite of all that, our wedding night was an absolute disaster! We both felt that somehow everything was wrong. She was scared and I was uncomfortable. Afterwards, we both felt awful—kind of guilty and kind of angry. It's gotten a little better since then, but not much. We both feel betrayed; no one told us it would be like this."

The three of us spent some time discussing a number of specifics about their courtship. Their approach to sexuality was the opposite extreme of most couples I've talked with. Their sexual commitment to each other was to have their first kiss on the wedding night. They had decided to avoid all physical contact until their vows were formalized in marriage.

TOTAL ABSTINENCE BEFORE MARRIAGE

I've encountered a number of engaged couples who have approached their sexual involvement from this perspective. Like Bob and Jane, they are usually committed, well-intentioned, and fairly self-disciplined Christians. Their logic makes sense. "If we're going to spend our lives together, there will be plenty of time for sex. If we aren't going to get married, why get started?"

Josh McDowell, in his study of sexual attitudes of teens, also encountered this approach among those he surveyed. In his book, *Why Wait?* he published several letters from young people which reflect this commitment.

> "I have made a commitment not to have any kind of physical relationship with a man before I'm married. Not even kissing. It seems odd to people in this day and age, because sex is taken so lightly and kissing is just for fun. But how can I think thoughts that are 'pure and honorable and lovely' (Philippians 4:8) when I am pressed close to someone's chest? How can I possibly set my mind on 'things above' (Colossians 3:2) when someone's mouth feels so warm on mine?"

In another letter, a young person expressed a similar commitment:

> "Abstinence is the best preventative. Refraining from even nominal physical contact until permanent commitment has been made may be the best for you."[8]

I won't debate the logic behind Bob and Jane's decision. If a couple decides to handle their physical relationship this way, I strongly encourage them to maintain their convictions. However, there are some hazards to this approach.

Strong warnings against sexual promiscuity may give the impression that the opposite must necessarily be true—if uncontrolled sexual liberty is bad, total physical abstinence must be great! If we take this reasoning to its logical conclusion, the ideal lifestyle would be that of a priest or monk—committed to celibacy for life, involved only in purely spiritual pursuits. Sometimes this seems like the only reasonable alternative to the problem. This is what the disciples suggested to Jesus when He explained the significance of divorce to them in Matthew 19. His response was interesting. He pointed out that not everyone could handle the single lifestyle but ". . . only those to whom it has been given" (Matthew 19:11). The implication is that for most of us, celibacy is probably not the solution. Somewhere there must be a balanced course of healthy sexual development and expression for individuals as well as couples.

Remember that sexual desire and involvement follow a natural progression in a relationship. Let's say that, for the couple planning to marry, the progression begins with holding hands and ends with sexual intercourse after the wedding. The process is, of course, much more complex than that, but to illustrate it in graph form would look like this:

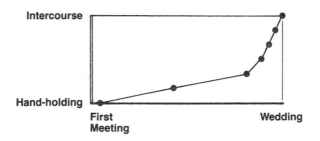

73

From the time a couple begins a relationship until the time of their marriage, sexual progression struggles for physical expression. (The implications of that expression happening too early in the relationship have been thoroughly discussed earlier in this book.) If we assume that the couple's goal is to eventually marry (which is not always the case) then the graph for those couples may look like this, which shows physical involvement progressing so quickly that intercourse occurs before the wedding. Here is where so many of the problem patterns have their start.

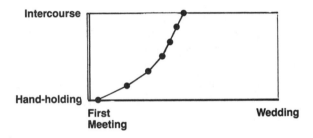

For a couple who have decided to abstain from the expression of physical affection, like Bob and Jane, the graph would look like this:

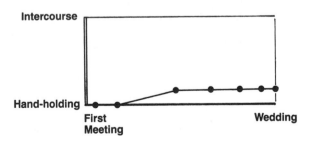

Here the concept of "premature consummation" is introduced. Premature consummation refers to the difference between the emotional development of a couple's physical relationship and their expectations for intercourse. In other words, a couple may not be emotionally ready for intercourse even though they have just been married. I need to emphasize that premature consummation is not a legal issue or a moral issue, it is an emotional issue. Premature consummation takes place when emotional development has been short-circuited.

PROBLEMS WITH PREMATURE CONSUMMATION

We have already said that sexual involvement is progressive. It is also a fact that our biological and emotional functions aren't always controlled by logical reasoning. Since these two things are true, it may be unrealistic to assume that something which has been treated as absolutely taboo for years (premarital sex) can be automatically reversed 180 degrees and experienced as absolutely wonderful a few hours after the wedding. Our minds may say yes, but chances are good that our emotions will say no. Young couples may experience guilt and fear even when there is nothing to feel guilty or fearful about. While there is nothing legal, moral, or scriptural to base these emotions on, the feelings are experienced just the same. The natural process of bonding needs to be recognized and respected. Short-cutting the process results in emotional and relational problems.

There are additional factors that may make the wedding night less than enjoyable for couples like Bob and Jane. For example, the first intercourse is often painful for the woman. That pain, coupled with the tension and apprehension of such a major switch in perspective, response, and behavior can make for a very negative experience. It's also possible that the new husband may be unaware of his bride's needs and desires. He may have trouble controlling how soon he comes to climax himself. All of these factors complicated Bob and Jane's experience, and started their sexual relationship with a load of negative emotions.

DELAYED CONSUMMATION

My suggestion to premarital couples with convictions similar to Bob and Jane's is this: If you mutually choose this route of avoiding all romantic physical contact prior to marriage, please don't let *anyone* convince you that you *must* have intercourse on your wedding night. I know many couples who would have developed a healthier and happier sexual relationship if they had not been in such a hurry to consummate their union on the wedding night. Weariness, frustration, tension, fear, ignorance—all have the potential to make the experience a miserable one.

Here are some suggestions to help you side-step some of these potential problems. Begin by having a discussion shortly before your wedding day. Talk openly and honestly about what would be most comfortable for each of you. It may feel awkward at first, but it will save you years of regret and painful memories. Following this discussion, set your limits as a couple according to the more modest of the two of you. This means that if the husband feels comfortable caressing his wife's body but she feels comfortable with only kissing, agree to go no farther than kissing for now. Allow her to become comfortable with the progression at her own pace. It is perfectly acceptable to move through the stages of kissing, French kissing, petting, and fondling before intercourse during the days and weeks after the wedding. If you move through the stages as they feel comfortable, you will enjoy complete sexual intimacy much more than you would have on your wedding night. In terms of our sexual expression graph, this progression would look like this:

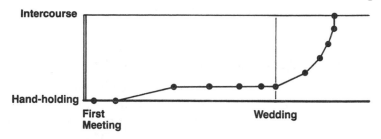

Intercourse

Hand-holding

First
Meeting

Wedding

In his book, *Solomon on Sex*, Joseph Dillow gives an excellent suggestion for couples like Bob and Jane who prefer to move more slowly and modestly in their sexual relationship.

> Let the new bride get into the bath first while the husband is in the other room. A candle lit in the bathroom, being the only light, will produce a warm, romantic atmosphere. As they relax together in the bathtub, they can discuss the day, talk and even pray thanking the Lord for the gift of each other. As they communicate and share, the warm water drains away the tensions of the day and the bubbles sufficiently hide the wife's body so she is not immediately embarrassed. They should then begin to gently stimulate each other under the water, hidden by the bubble bath! As the sexual tension and anticipation mounts, many of the initial inhibitions begin to melt away and a transfer to the bedroom is more natural.[9]

There are many other creative ways to overcome inhibition, but the most important elements are these: Relax, talk openly about your feelings, and let things progress at the rate that is most comfortable for both of you. Make it an adventure of discovering each other. And, oh yes, please be ready to laugh at yourselves and *with* one another when things don't go as smoothly as they do in the movies (because they almost never do!) It will give you stories to laugh about for years . . . though you may never get to tell them to anyone else!

MISUNDERSTANDING GOD'S VIEW OF SEX

For some couples, sexual abstinence is not the result of a mutual decision. Frequently it is the result of ignorance, misbelief, and a misunderstanding of God's intention for married love. Such was the case of Tim and Judy.

Both Tim and Judy came from families with very strict moral standards. Both families were missionaries in northern Africa where Tim and Judy met as children. Neither considered their families affectionate—hugs and kisses were seldom exchanged between family members. Tim could not remember the topic of sex ever being mentioned at home. The only discussion of sex that Judy had been exposed to while growing up revolved around the dangerous sins of lust and fornication.

When Tim and Judy came back to the U.S. to attend Bible college, each found very few friends who shared their conservative views. So they were naturally attracted to each other and were married shortly after graduation.

When they made an appointment for counseling they had been married almost a year. During our first session it became clear that they had not yet experienced sexual intercourse. Tim felt frustrated and vaguely guilty for his sexual desire toward his bride. Whenever he brought up the subject Judy pointed out that they were not yet ready to have children, and she made comments questioning his spirituality. Tim had stopped bringing up the topic but was bothered by lustful thoughts, guilt, and resentment.

In several sessions I carefully showed Tim and Judy how God views sex in marriage, and they eventually realized that they needed to work on revamping their views about sex to coincide with Scripture.

Tim and Judy had projected their own ideas onto God. They had become familiar with bits and pieces of Scripture that supported the message they assumed to be there.

I've heard several well-meaning Christians teach that the sex act is a result of Adam's sin. They believe that when Adam brought sin to the human race by eating forbidden fruit, part of that sin was sexual intercourse. Take a look at the first chapter of the book of Genesis. Read the whole chapter, then focus in on verse 28:

> *God blessed them and said to them, "Be fruitful and increase in number; fill the earth and subdue it. Rule over the fish of the sea and the birds of the air and over every living creature that moves on the ground."*

God is telling Adam and Eve to increase in number, and that means sex, folks! Unless God has made some significant changes in human anatomy that He didn't tell us about, sex for Adam and Eve was basically the same as it is for us today.

The sin of Adam and the subsequent fall of man doesn't occur until the third chapter of Genesis. This tells us that God created and ordained the sex act *before* sin entered the world. So much for sex being inherently bad. Now take a look at verse 31:

> *God saw all that he had made, and it was very good. And there was evening, and there was morning—the sixth day.*

When God says that *everything* He made was *very* good, He's including sex in the package. He is including all of man's and woman's anatomy in that statement. This has some interesting implications. A brief study of the female anatomy will reveal a small organ called the clitoris. It is located just above the vagina. The clitoris has a large number of nerve endings and is extremely responsive to touch. The interesting thing is that there is no discernible function for the clitoris except physical stimulation and arousal. This indicates that the clitoris was created by God with no other purpose than sexual pleasure. That tells us quite a bit about God's view of sex.

Think about it . . . *after* creating the sex act, *after* creating all parts of human sexual anatomy, "God saw all that He had made and it was *very* good." If you read Genesis 2:25, you'll see that Adam and Eve felt pretty good about it too. God always intended for sex to be good, clean fun.

The Bible promotes and encourages sex within the stability of a marriage commitment, never outside of it. Within the loving marriage commitment God gives no sexual restrictions at all.

This is difficult for many Christians to accept because their sexual drives seem to be condemned by Paul's statements about "the lusts of the flesh." In this way, many Christians actually manufacture restrictions that seem godly to them. In reality, most only serve to limit their fulfillment. In chapter 9 we will take a closer look at what God has said about sexuality.

Tim and Judy began to discover the positive side of God's gift of sex through their own study of the Bible. They began to understand and experience the exciting freedom of the physical love God intended for married couples. For them marriage became an exciting adventure they never knew was possible.

GROWING CLOSER

1) If you were to choose to avoid any physical involvement prior to marriage, how would your friends react? How would your family respond?

How do you usually respond to peer pressure: compromise, withdrawal, or consistency?

How do you think your decision would be affected by your friends' and/or family members' reactions?

2) If you've made a decision to delay physical involvement, how do you believe your past relationships have affected this decision?

3) In what ways would you like to prepare for your first sexual experience with your marriage partner?

For a more thorough treatment of the subject, you may want to read:

David Hocking, *Romantic Lovers* (Eugene, Ore.: Harvest House, 1987).

Joseph Dillow, *Solomon on Sex* (Nashville, Tenn.: Thomas Nelson Publishers, 1977).

In a culture that promotes sexual activity as intensely as ours does, we have carefully avoided discussing the dangers which go hand in hand with the lifestyle.

6

THE
DOUBLE-EDGED TRAP

S arah came to my office anxious and preoccupied. As a working single parent, she had a great deal to think about even without her current crisis: Her sixteen-year-old daughter, Julie, had just given birth to a five-pound girl. Life was about to change drastically for all of them.

This situation was not new to Sarah. Her own mother had been pregnant before she was married. That marriage lasted for a miserable thirty-five years. The entire family still suffers from it, though the children are all grown and Sarah's father died several years earlier. Even so, her oldest brother, Glenn, still bitterly expressed his resentment over being the cause and victim of that disastrous marriage.

Sarah married Tom after finding out she was pregnant. At eighteen years of age she was anxious to get away from her parents, and she fell madly in love with Tom. Looking back, she realizes that neither of them was ready for marriage. Tom left two years after their daughter was born and Sarah hasn't heard from him since.

Now the pattern had repeated itself in a third generation. "I can't get Julie to understand how serious this is," Sarah was saying. "Her boyfriend is denying that it's his child and will have nothing to do with Julie now. She keeps saying that everything will be fine, but she doesn't see how much better it *could* have been." Sarah's emotions seemed to turn off as she continued, "I was planning to take some computer classes next semester. I was hoping to get promoted and finally have a little extra cash. Now all that will have to wait for at least a few years. I was hoping that Julie could go to college and have a better life than we've had, but that isn't likely now. I don't think we can afford much day-care. I'll probably need to cut back at work to make sure the baby is cared for. That way Julie can at least finish high school."

The trauma of unwanted pregnancy is often underestimated by most young people. Unwed mothers in the U.S. number well over one million annually. Each year over thirty thousand girls under age fifteen become mothers. Some studies estimate that 40 percent of today's fourteen-year-old girls will become pregnant before they are twenty years old.[10]

These are staggering statistics! The negative effects of these patterns are monumental to our nation, to our families, to the next generation, and most importantly, to the unwed mothers and their children.

The majority of young mothers in the U.S. live below the poverty level. Only one-half of these girls who give birth before age eighteen complete high school (96 percent of girls without children finish high school in the U.S.). Seventy-one percent of women under age thirty who receive welfare had their first child before age twenty. This pattern of unwed childbirth is often called the "hub of the U.S. poverty cycle." The Center for Population Options estimates that ten years ago the cost of welfare support to unwed mothers in America was $8 billion. In 1986, the cost was $17 billion and continues to rise.[11]

The babies of unwed mothers have extremely high rates of illness and death. As they grow they're far more likely to experience educational, emotional, and behavioral problems than other children. The rate of child abuse among these children is far above the national average.

It would seem that the most immediate answer to the problem of unwanted pregnancy is the use of contraceptives. During the last twenty years, contraceptives have been developed, improved, promoted, and distributed. Today, over-the-counter contraceptives such as condoms, foams, and sponges are available to anyone of any age. However, after over two decades of having freely available contraceptives, the problem of unwanted pregnancies is no better. Most statistics indicate that the problem is significantly worse than twenty-five years ago.

The major problem with contraceptive use among single people is that they are used irresponsibly or not at all. The prevalent attitude in our culture seems to be counterproductive to itself. There is a double standard that exists among singles regarding sexual activity. On one hand, virginity is considered immature and unsophisticated. At the same time, *preplanned* illicit sex is somehow immoral. To be swept away by passion is understandable, forgivable, and even desirable, but to plan ahead for sex by using a contraceptive is considered bad. One teenager interviewed in *Psychology Today* expressed the attitude well when she said, "If I did [use a contraceptive] then I'd have sex more. Then it would be too easy. . . . I don't feel it's right. I haven't been raised that way."[12]

This attitude is strongly substantiated by the people

I counsel. I am surprised by the number of single people who are supposedly "sophisticated" and sexually "liberated" who, when they are really honest, experience a deep sense of guilt over the use of contraceptives. This seems to be especially true of women who want to avoid the stigma of being "loose" or "available." The trouble is that when you're taking a pill every day or carrying a diaphragm in your purse—"just in case"—sooner or later you will have to face the fact that these terms apply to you.

Of course, most people don't like to think of themselves as statistics. Most sexually active singles don't plan on getting pregnant, though they seldom use contraceptives. Most single pregnant women expected, or at least hoped, that they would beat the odds. There are certainly exceptions to the statistics, but exceptions are rare. The single woman who discovers that she is pregnant has four options open to her. Whichever one she chooses will profoundly change her life and the lives of many other people. She may: 1) Marry in order to provide a two-parent home for the child; 2) Raise the child alone (perhaps marry in the future); 3) Abort the child before birth; 4) place the child up for adoption. Let's take a look at some of the consequences of these options.

PREMATURE MARRIAGES

In most instances, marriage because of pregnancy creates serious problems. A couple's developing relationship is short-circuited as they are forced into parental roles they have not anticipated or prepared for. They often start resenting each other and the child. Behind that resentment are almost always deep feelings of failure and frustration at having to change life plans, goals, and ideals. The needs of the child compounded with the needs of each partner result in demands that are greater than most young relationships can bear.

These marriages do not always end in divorce, but communication is seldom well developed, or if it was good at one time, it usually deteriorates. Conflicts often are not resolved, and the potential for unfaithfulness in both partners is multiplied. Resentment, regret, and guilt become an inherent part of the marriage. Everyone loses. The biggest loss of all is experienced by the innocent child born without choice or preparation into this situation. While professional therapy can be extremely beneficial for these marriages, most young couples don't seek counseling.

UNWED PARENTHOOD

While there are exceptions, usually the fathers involved in premarital pregnancies are absent, uninvolved, or disinterested. A generation ago it was assumed that a couple would marry if the woman was pregnant. Though the resulting marriage was usually less than satisfying, the emphasis was on responsibility, not satisfaction. Today, unmarried fathers seldom contribute financially to their children's support.

A study by the Guttmacher Institute, published in *Psychology Today,* showed that families headed by young mothers are seven times more likely to be living below the poverty line than other families.[13] Some of the resulting hardships are reflected in the statistics quoted at the beginning of this chapter. Besides the financial hardships, the individuals involved often have a very unrealistic concept of motherhood (or fatherhood). Even in an ideal marriage, time, patience, energy, and hard work are necessary to care for a child. Add financial strain, loss of a relationship, change in life plans, fears of dependency, feelings of abandonment, guilt, and failure, and you can begin to see the complexity of unwed parenthood.

Often forgotten in the statistics are the grandparents of the new baby, although they figure very significantly in the picture. Frequently the pregnant woman's parents end up in a role of support they hadn't planned on and may resent. Their own dreams must die if they desire to adequately support their daughter.

Sometimes competition develops between grandparent and mother as to "who knows best" and who raises the child. The feelings of the new mother toward her parents are mixed. It's not unusual for her to feel a blend of gratitude and resentment. This causes additional strain at a time when energy and patience are low for everyone involved.

THE ABORTION DECEPTION

Sadly, in our society abortion is another option for the unwed mother. As controversial as the issue is, it is the option chosen in an overwhelming number of cases. This year more than one million teenage girls will become pregnant. That's over three thousand every day! Almost one-half of these girls will have abortions.

In a recent poll, 56 percent of high school students and 50 percent of college students felt that abortion was the best solution to an unwanted pregnancy.[14] This correlates with a number of studies which show that 50 percent of unwanted pregnancies in the U.S. end in abortion. This mass murder of unborn human beings is a sad commentary on our society's values. I'm convinced this atrocity will be recognized by the next generation and they will mourn the death of these children.

The frightening aspect of these statistics is that the consequences of abortion are significantly misrepresented, minimized, or ignored by abortion's supporters and are seldom presented to the prospective mother.

Abortion is viewed by many as no more than a simple medical procedure! This is so far from the truth. Emotional and spiritual trauma is the rule rather than the exception for the would-be mother.

A study by Dr. Anne Speckhard, cited in *Why Wait?* by Josh McDowell, shows many of the long-term (five to ten years later) emotional consequences of abortion. Of the women interviewed in that study:

81% reported preoccupation with the aborted child

73% reported flashbacks of the abortion experience

69% reported feelings of "craziness" after the abortion

54% recalled nightmares related to the abortion

35% reported visitations from the aborted child

23% reported hallucinations related to the abortion.

In Dr. Speckhard's findings, 72 percent of the subjects said they held no religious beliefs at the time of their abortions and *96 percent* in retrospect regarded abortion as the taking of life or as murder.[15]

Abortion is far more than a medical procedure or a political issue. Abortion has profound effects—emotional, psychological, and spiritual—that must not be ignored. While a thorough evaluation of the topic is beyond the scope of this book, there are many fine books that deal with it. One I recommend is *Abortion's Second Victim* by Pam Koerbel, published by Victor Books. The author does a very thorough job of explaining some of the popular notions and myths surrounding abortion. She offers personal insight for those who need help in healing with the hurts associated with abortion.

THE ADOPTION OPTION

The long-range consequences of adoption tend to be fewer and less severe than the other options. It is often the most positive option because it generally provides a loving home for the child as well as medical care and emotional support for the mother. However, adoption is by no means an easy decision to make. Mothers who have given their newborn child to adoptive parents generally express a deep feeling of loss. There is a period of grieving as normal and expected as there would be in any significant experience of loss.

Premarital pregnancy, with its far-reaching and tragic consequences, is only half of a double-edged "blade." The other edge is just as devastating and can be a deadly reminder of wrong choices.

SEXUALLY TRANSMITTED DISEASES

Premarital sex always carries the threat of sexually transmitted disease (STD). The impact of this trap, like that of pregnancy, goes far beyond the sexually involved couple. Friends, family, and future sexual partners are deeply affected as are the children born diseased and deformed by STDs. Also affected is the medical community which treats the massive number of cases each year, as well as the insurance industry and welfare system which pay for that treatment. Our society suffers profoundly from the effects of this sexual trap—the result of people making individual decisions regarding sexual standards.

Karen was an attractive, single, twenty-four-year-old flight attendant. Though she was very popular socially and had many boyfriends, she had been involved sexually only twice, both times with men she cared for deeply.

"I can't believe it!" Karen's words could hardly be understood through her sobbing. "I just can't believe it.

Why would God let this happen? What am I going to do?"

A few hours before our discussion, her family doctor had diagnosed her as having contracted genital herpes. She understood that there was no remedy for the disease, and that potentially she would pass the incurable malady on for the remainder of her life to any person with whom she shared herself sexually. The desperation of her words still echo in my memory: "What healthy Christian man is going to risk marriage with me now? If only . . ."

Every day thousands of individuals contract a sexually transmitted disease. For them there are no quiet words of reassurance to make the problem go away. The term *STD* rather than *venereal disease* is used here because a number of the diseases discussed in this chapter are also transmitted by means other than sexual contact.

Many of these diseases are occurring in epidemic proportions. According to an estimate by the American Social Health Association, someone in America contracts a sexually transmitted disease every three seconds. Roughly thirty thousand new cases of STDs are reported every day. In fact, after the common cold, gonorrhea and syphilis are two of the most common infectious diseases in the United States. This is no small problem, considering the possible effects. Several of the STDs have no cure or even treatment. Many end in death.

As I talk with people in my practice, as well as in my teaching, I am often amazed at their ignorance concerning these diseases. In a culture which promotes sexual activity as intensely as ours does, we have carefully avoided discussing the obvious dangers and health hazards which go hand in hand with the lifestyle. To some degree, the results of that ignorance are the diseases discussed in this chapter.

By no means will this be an exhaustive text of all health hazards related to sexual behavior. It is meant only to be a brief description and reference for the major or most common of the sexually transmitted diseases. If you have any of the symptoms described here, of if you have any reason to believe you've contracted an STD, consult your doctor and explain your fears. Don't hesitate; not one of these diseases is worth ignoring.

If some of the terms and descriptions are unclear to you, I recommend reading *Intended for Pleasure* by Dr. Ed Wheat for illustrations and descriptions of the functioning of male and female reproductive systems.

Gonorrhea

Known in street language as "clap," gonorrhea is caused by a bacteria called "Neisseria gonorrhoeae." This disease infects over two million people each year, and more than half of the reported infections in the United States involve people under twenty-five years of age.

Since the bacteria cannot survive outside of warm mucus membranes, it is practically impossible to contract the disease from toilet seats, towels, drinking glasses, etc. The disease is transmitted by sexual contact. Evidence does not seem to indicate that it can be transmitted through kissing alone.

Symptoms: Some men (10 percent) and most women (80 percent) experience no symptoms at all until the disease has severely damaged their reproductive organs. For most women, the disease is not detected until it has reached this advanced stage. The most common symptoms, when apparent, are:

In men - In the early stages, burning sensation during urination and/or cloudy discharge from the penis. In the latter stages, swelling at the base of the testicle and/or inflammation of the scrotal skin.

In women - In the early stages, some green or yellowish discharge, though this is rarely heavy. In the latter stages, pelvic inflammatory disease.

Treatment: Gonorrhea is generally treated with penicillin or, for people allergic to penicillin, with tetracycline or erythromycin. Most people respond well to treatment if the problem is diagnosed early enough. About 10 percent of cases, however, are more resistant and require extensive treatment.

In the 1970s a new strain of gonorrhea bacteria emerged that is stronger than the older strains and resistant to penicillin. It is believed that this strain developed in Southeast Asia as a result of the use of black market penicillin in low doses by Vietnamese prostitutes. These low doses of weak penicillin killed only the weak organisms and allowed the stronger bacteria to survive and develop a tolerance to penicillin. In these cases other medication must be developed and used.

Complications: As mentioned earlier, 80 percent of women have no observable symptoms until the reproductive organs are significantly involved. Since this is true, it is common for women to spread the disease to sexual partners without knowing it. At least half of the women who remain untreated for two or more months are infected throughout the vagina, cervix, uterus, and fallopian tubes. The bacteria spreads very quickly during menstruation. It is usually not until the bacteria leaks out of the fallopian tubes into the abdominal cavity and onto the ovaries that noticeable symptoms occur. At this point it is known as pelvic inflammatory disease (PID). The symptoms of PID include disrupted menstrual cycles, high temperature, headache, vomiting, pain in the lower abdomen, and, in 20 to 30 percent of women, sterilization.

Often scar tissue forms in the fallopian tubes, partially blocking the tube. When this happens, a sperm cell may bypass a partially blocked area and fertilize an ovum which consequently cannot reach the uterus through the blocked area. The result is a tubal pregnancy which is a very serious health hazard for the woman. It will require an abortion of the fertilized ovum for the protection of the mother's life.

A child born to a woman infected with gonorrhea may contract gonococcal eye infection from the birth canal. Generally, silver nitrate drops applied at birth prevent serious complications for the child. There are a few cases where adults have contracted gonococcal eye infection by touching their eyes immediately after handling their genitals.

Oral contact with infected genitals may transmit the bacteria to the throat.

Syphilis

This is a very serious STD, though less common than gonorrhea. There are approximately 100,000 new cases reported in the United States each year. Syphilis is caused by a thin, corkscrewlike organism called a "spirochete" (Latin—*treponema pallidum*). Like the gonorrhea bacteria, the spirochete requires a warm, moist environment to survive. Therefore, it is almost always contracted through sexual contact. The organism is passed from open lesions of an infected person to the mucus membranes or openings in the skin of a sexual partner. Syphilis is one of the STDs that may result in death.

Symptoms: The disease progresses through four stages of development.

First Stage - A small, painless sore or "chanchre" appears at the site of infection where the spirochete entered the body, usually in the genital area or mouth. Because the sore is small and painless, it often goes unnoticed. The chanchre will generally heal in one to five weeks. After it heals, there are typically no symptoms of syphilis for several weeks, although the individual can still infect a sexual partner. After several weeks of remaining dormant, the disease progresses to the second stage.

Second Stage - During this stage, a skin rash develops on the body. This rash usually does not hurt or itch. For some people, the rash is rarely noticeable; for others, it is very evident with hard, raised bumps.

If the individual doesn't seek treatment at this stage, the rash will generally heal in a few weeks. At this point the disease enters the very dangerous third stage.

Third Stage - This stage is called the "latent stage" of syphilis, during which there may be no visible symptoms for several years. The organisms, however, continue to multiply. After one year in the latent stage the individual usually is no longer contagious to sexual partners. However, if a woman with syphilis at any stage is pregnant, she can pass the disease on to her unborn infant through the placental blood system.

Fourth Stage - The final stage of syphilis is extremely serious and often results in death. The symptoms may appear anywhere from three to forty years after the initial infection. These symptoms may include blindness, skin ulcers, paralysis, ruptured blood vessels, liver damage, heart failure, and severe mental disturbances.

Treatment: The treatment for syphilis is virtually the same as that for gonorrhea. Generally, penicillin is used unless an individual is allergic to it, in which case some other antibiotic is given. Since there are often no symptoms evident in syphilis, an individual should have several blood tests after treatment to be sure he is free of the organism.

Complications: As mentioned earlier, an infected pregnant woman can pass the disease on to her unborn child. Syphilis can cause extreme damage or death to infected newborns after the first trimester of pregnancy. Therefore, it is very important for any woman with even a remote possibility of infection to be tested during the first three months of pregnancy.

Chlamydia Trachomatis

Caused by a one-celled organism called the "trichomonas vaginalis," it is the most common STD in women. It is estimated by some experts that one in four women are infected, though not all infected woman show overt symptoms.

The organism can survive outside the body for several hours in a moist environment. It is possible to contract the disease from a towel, wash cloth, toilet seat, or other object used by an infected person when it comes in close contact with an individual's genitals. However, it is generally transmitted through genital sexual contact.

Symptoms: In women the symptoms are usually a frothy white or yellow discharge, which has an unpleasant odor, from the vagina. This is often accompanied by sore, inflamed, and itchy tissue in the vagina. Occasionally the disease affects the bladder or Bartholin's glands.

In men there are rarely any observable symptoms. Occasionally there is a white discharge from the penis accompanied by a burning or itching sensation.

Treatment: Chlamydia is usually treated by administering the prescription drug metronidazole (also called flagyl). Treatment generally takes ten to fourteen days to be effective.

Complications: The treatment prescription, metronidazole, has been linked to cancer, and its use should be discussed with a physician before it is administered. Also, if alcohol is consumed during the drug administration, undesirable side effects can result. Without treatment, long-term infection with this disease may damage the cells of the cervix and promote cervical cancer.

Genital Warts

These are warts which are passed through sexual contact and appear in the genital area. They are caused by a virus similar to that producing warts on other parts of the body. Approximately one million cases are reported each year.

Symptoms: The warts generally do not appear until about three months after contact with an infected person. When they appear in moist areas, they are soft and pink or red with an appearance similar to that of cauliflower. When they appear in dry areas, they are hard and yellow-gray.

Treatment: When the warts are small, they are treated with an application of podophyllum, a dark resinlike medication. The podophyllum is applied to the surface of the wart and left on for six hours. Generally, several treatments are required. Surgical removal of large warts may be necessary.

Complications: There is some evidence linking genital warts to cervical cancer in women. Also, in childbirth, the infant may contract the disease while passing through the birth canal. In the infant, the warts may appear internally, such as in the throat or lungs.

Genital Herpes

This is an STD caused by a virus called herpes simplex. There are two types of herpes virus. Type 1 generally is manifested in cold sores or blisters in the mouth, lips or nose, and seldom in the genital area. Type 2 generally causes sores in the genital area, though occasionally may cause a cold sore or blister in the mouth. Type 2 is the virus to be discussed here.

This virus currently affects five to twenty million people in the U.S., with 200,000 to 500,000 new cases reported each year. Herpes is spread through sexual contact, kissing, and touching active sores. The virus can survive for several hours on objects such as towels, drinking glasses, and toilet seats. Experts say that contracting herpes from those sources is possible, though rare.

Symptoms: One or more bumps or "papules" form in the genital area. They appear generally between two and eight days after contact with an infected individual, though they may appear as much as twenty days after sexual exposure. They are fairly painful. These papules soon form blisters filled with a clear fluid containing the virus. This fluid is extremely infectious and turns to pus as the body's white blood cells attack the virus. When the blisters rupture to form wet, painful open sores, the disease is at its most contagious stage. The sores eventually form a crust and begin to heal. This healing may take as long as ten days.

Other common symptoms of genital herpes are swollen glands, muscle aches, fever, and pain on urination. Often the victims cannot walk or sit. The symptoms can last four to six weeks.

Even after healing, the virus does not go away. Once an individual is infected, he or she is infected for life. The virus retreats up the nerve fibers and rests in the nerve cells adjacent to the lower spinal cord. Often there are periodic recurrences of the symptoms as the virus returns down the fibers to the genitals.

Treatment: There is, at this point in time, no treatment known for the herpes virus. Most treatments are designed to relieve pain and discomfort during an outbreak. Usually a topical analgesic is applied to the infected area.

Complications: There are two possible complications to herpes in women. First, the risk of developing cancer of the cervix is five to eight times higher in women who have genital herpes than in the general population. Second, a newborn child is almost sure to be infected with genital herpes while passing through the birth canal. Usually, when this risk is high, caesarean section is performed to minimize risk to the child. Almost 65 percent of infected newborns will either be severely disabled or die.

Touching herpes sores is extremely dangerous. The virus spreads easily and quickly to adjacent areas. It is important for both the infected individual as well as others to avoid touching the sores. By touching a sore, the infected individual may convey the infection to other parts of his body. This particular problem has resulted in serious eye damage in many cases where the eyes were touched after the sores were touched. Recent studies indicate that genital herpes may be transmitted even when *no* symptoms occur.

Acquired Immune Deficiency Syndrome (AIDS)

First identified in 1981, there is still much to learn about AIDS. It is predicted that it could become the leading cause of death in this country by the early 1990s. The AIDS virus destroys the body's ability to ward off infection. It is spread primarily through sexual contact and the exchange of body fluids. It is also spread by sharing IV (intravenous) needles. Although debated by some, there is evidence that casual contact will not transmit the virus—sharing bathrooms; sharing silverware, dishes, or glasses; coughing, sneezing, shaking hands, or hugging. *Campus Life* magazine recently reported, "According to the Centers for Disease Control, more than 20,000 people have died of AIDS. Another 35,000 have developed the disease, and another 100,000 to 300,000 are showing some symptoms. An estimated 1.2 million to 1.5 million people carry the virus, but have yet to show any symptoms. Between 25 and 50 percent of those carrying the virus are expected to get AIDS in the next seven years."[16]

Symptoms: Because AIDS has a long latency period (usually five to seven years), there may be no early symptoms immediately after the disease is contracted. Following the latency period, there is a broad range of symptoms including: swollen lymph glands, fatigue, malaise, fever, night sweats, diarrhea, weight loss, and Kaposi's sarcoma, a form of cancer. Often there are mental and neurological problems as the virus begins to invade the brain cells. Forgetfulness, impaired speech, tremors, and seizures gradually increase in severity.

Treatment: At the present time there is no known cure and no effective treatment for AIDS. No one has ever been known to recover.

Complications: Although in the past the disease has risen faster in the homosexual and drug-using sections of the population, "the occurrences of the disease are [now] rising fastest among heterosexuals. By 1991, heterosexuals will account for an estimated 5 percent, up from 1.5 percent in 1984. No definitive cure or vaccine has been found; projections run as high as 1.1 million cases by 1997."[17]

All of the diseases we have discussed in this chapter are extremely dangerous and have become national health hazards. Research will continue, discoveries will be made, and most likely new diseases will develop; but most people do have a choice as to whether they will be exposed to these diseases.

There is only one solution to the tremendous problem of sexually transmitted diseases. That solution has a guaranteed 100 percent success rate. As a matter of fact, through it we can totally destroy most sexually transmitted diseases in one generation. It has been recognized for thousands of years, though never effectively carried out. As is true for each problem we've discussed in this book, the only realistic solution comes back to the clear biblical standard of marriage: one sexual partner, and a lifetime commitment to remain faithful and to share that part of the relationship with none other until the death of that partner. (Back in the "olden days" that was called morality and fidelity.) If that were the case, STDs would be gone by the time our grandchildren were eligible to worry about them.

The road to true sexual fulfillment is full of potholes and dead-end detours. But there is a road map, clear and definite. If we follow that map, even if we'd like to take the detour that "feels" right at the moment, we will reach our destination.

GROWING CLOSER

If you are unmarried:

1)   What would life be like in your home if a new-born baby became a part of it? Describe it in as much detail as possible.

2)   What dreams for the future would you need to give up? What dreams would you need to modify? How?

If your marriage began in pregnancy:

1)   How would your marital relationship be different had the pregnancy occurred after the wedding?

2)   What *specifically* is keeping your marriage from developing these positive aspects now?

3)   Do you need to forgive someone in order to make these adjustments?

Do you need to forgive yourself?

Read John 8:1-11. Make some decisions regarding how you will respond to past mistakes, both your own and those of others.

The most frightening aspect of his problem was that no one suspected. He had become an expert at covering up.

7

SEXUAL ADDICTION

This chapter is not about sinful behavior, though sinful behavior will be discussed. It is not about overindulgence in sex, although sex is certainly involved. This chapter is about a sickness. It is a sickness of mind and spirit that by its very nature keeps people from getting well. Unlike physical illness, here the individual is personally responsible for both the symptoms and the cure. It is a sickness to which Christians are not immune. It is about an addiction—an addiction to lust. It is more prevalent than most people could imagine. Both men and women are equally subject to sexual addiction. I have chosen to use the pronouns "he" and "him" in this chapter only to preserve sentence continuity.

Think about chemical addiction for a moment. When an individual is addicted to alcohol or some other drug, that drug becomes a preoccupation. The addict will go to great lengths to satisfy his craving for it. The substance will become more important than family, friends, or work. Eventually the drug is needed to feel normal. The addict's life becomes unmanageable as important relationships are sacrificed for the addiction.

Now transfer that description into the sexual area and we're talking about sexual addiction. A clinical definition is, "A pathological relationship with a mood-altering experience which becomes the central focus of attention."[18] An addict's judgment is significantly impaired and he pursues his addiction in spite of serious negative consequences.

JUST OVERSEXED?

Before Steve married, his reputation was that of a playboy. He was handsome and athletic and had no trouble finding women who wanted to spend time with him. His relationships were invariably short-term and sexual. For Steve, the prospect of a "conquest" was exhilarating, though he seemed to have little desire for a relationship beyond physical involvement. In fact, many of his relationships were with women whom he didn't particularly like. His friends were amazed at his ability to have another girlfriend "lined up" whenever a relationship would dissolve.

Inwardly, Steve often longed for a relationship that was more than just sexual. At times his feelings of loneliness were overwhelming. He periodically decided that the next time he would move slower, be less aggressive physically; but it never changed. He always seemed to follow the same pattern and his relationships never lasted long. After becoming sexually involved with a woman, he soon found himself feeling closed-in, and he wanted to escape.

At times it had crossed Steve's mind that something might be wrong but he would quickly dismiss the thought. He rationalized his behavior to himself by thinking that he was just naturally affectionate and had a very strong sex drive. This seemed to be confirmed by the fact that he felt the need to masturbate in spite of a sexual relationship with his girlfriends.

When Steve met Ann, something seemed to change. He felt differently toward her than any of his previous girlfriends. Though he still enjoyed their sexual relationship, he had a desire to be with her more than any other girl. After ten months of steady dating, Steve and Ann were married.

After the wedding Steve vowed to devote himself totally to Ann. After a few weeks, however, he began masturbating again. His job had become more stressful and Steve used this fact to justify his need for "release," as he called it. Within six months of their marriage, Steve began to secretly visit adult book stores and massage parlors. While he felt deeply guilty, he reminded himself of his "strong sex drive" and concluded that the most loving thing was to not burden Ann with it. Before long he was visiting prostitutes almost weekly.

After the birth of their son, Michael, Steve and Ann's sexual relationship slowed down for several months. Though their frequency of intercourse resumed before long, Steve spent two years justifying his compulsion by telling himself that he needed release and his wife wasn't available.

By this time Steve was living in two completely different worlds. One was a world of cheap motel rooms, adult book stores, and dingy massage parlors. The other was a warm, loving family who wanted to be close to him. Steve was aware of his feeling of loneliness even while he was with his wife and son. While he was single, the dichotomy between his addiction and the rest of his life was not so great He wasn't really close to anyone, and his addictive behavior was normalized and ignored by a permissive culture. His deep sense of isolation was hidden in sexual activity.

Steve had a natural ability to talk. People naturally trusted him. This gift made him very successful at his sales job. It also helped him cover up his compulsive behavior. He soon found himself caught up in a tangled web of lies and deceitful excuses. He would lie to his boss about missed sales meetings while "cruising" for prostitutes. He would lie to Ann for being late because of a visit to a porn shop. Once a client mentioned one of Steve's missed appointments to Ann and they discovered that Steve had told each a different story regarding his whereabouts. Through a complex series of excuses, Steve was able to extricate himself from even that situation. By this time he had become an accomplished liar. Steve was aware that he had become compulsive in ways he didn't want to be. His big fear was that he would be totally rejected and lose everything he valued if anyone found out.

Once, while shopping with Ann, Steve made a stop at the rest room specifically to masturbate. It was at this time that he began to recognize his sickness. He had an attractive, loving wife available to him, yet he chose to have sex with himself. This was the first crack in his shield of denial. Several times while contemplating his situation he wept in shame and regret. He promised himself he would stop, but soon became involved again, sometimes on the very same day as his resolution.

Once Steve read in the paper that the vice squad had raided a porn theater he frequented. The fact that he had been there two days before the raid sent a chill through him. He vowed never to attend another porn show. Within a month, however, he was back in that same theater.

The turning point came after a physical examination for work when he was diagnosed as having genital herpes.

Ann was devastated. Steve told her that it must have resulted from one impulsive incident at a convention several months earlier. He promised it was a mistake that would never reoccur. Ann said she needed time to think and took Michael, their son, to the coast for a few days to sort things out. While there, she thought a great deal about the patterns in their marriage and about Steve's continual excuses. She made phone calls to several of Steve's friends and co-workers, and after putting some of the facts together she concluded that Steve had been lying to her for a long time.

When Ann came home she presented Steve with an ultimatum: either he seek counseling or she would leave him. Steve was terrified of revealing his secret life, even to a counselor, but the cost of his compulsion was now too great. He agreed to therapy.

Steve spent two years in both individual and group therapy. During that time he discovered that there were many people with his problem. With the help of his therapist, his new friends, and the support of his wife, Steve was able to see things very differently. He discovered a relationship with Jesus Christ that he never knew was possible. The strength and security he found there gave him courage to make changes. It was never easy and is still in process. Now, Steve's secret life is more a sad memory than a terrifying fear.

In Steve's situation, he was willing to sacrifice everything for sexual satisfaction. He repeatedly risked job, marriage, family, friends, and self-respect. He continually promised himself that he would change, that it would never happen again. He found himself telling more and more lies to cover up his behavior. At times he lost track of what the truth was because of his many lies. His life was often on the verge of disaster because of his behavior. He hurt very deeply and was intensely lonely. He was aware that his sexual activity increased his pain and yet he continued in it.

In his book *Out of the Shadows*, Dr. Patrick Carnes describes the problem:

> The addict uses—or abuses rather—one of the most exciting moments in human experience: sex. Sexual arousal becomes intensified. The addict's mood is altered as he or she enters the obsessive trance. The metabolic responses are like a rush through the body as adrenalin speeds up the body's functioning. The heart pounds as the addict focuses on his search object. Risk, danger, and even violence are the ultimate escalators. One can always increase the dosage of intoxication. Preoccupation effectively buries the personal pain of remorse and regret. The addict does not always have to act. Often just thinking about it brings relief.
>
> The sexual addict's excitement-seeking parallels some other types of compulsive/obsessive addicts. In that sense, there is little difference between the voyeur waiting for hours by a window for ninety seconds of nudity and the compulsive gambler hunching on a long shot. What makes the sexual addict different is that he draws upon the human emotions generated by courtship and passion.[19]

The most frightening aspect of Steve's problem is that no one suspected. Not one of his friends or co-workers would have guessed that Steve led a secret life. He had become an expert at covering up.

DENIAL

A primary factor that allows an addict to continue an addiction is a defense mechanism called denial. Denial is more complex than simply telling a lie. Denial is the individual's ability to distort reality until no one recognizes the problem, including the addict himself. This is accomplished in many ways. Rationalizing, justifying, and ignoring the problem become so habitual that the denial can look and feel like reality. The following list will give some idea of the many forms denial may take. It is a list of common rationalizations used by sexual addicts to hide their problem, even from themselves:

- Everyone does it, just in different ways.
- If only my wife were more interested in sex.
- What he/she/they don't know won't hurt them.
- Anyone would do the same thing if they were in my situation.
- The pressure builds up and I need release.
- I couldn't stop myself, because of what she was doing.
- All women really want it, they just play games.
- After all, sex is man's strongest drive.
- Nobody's really getting hurt.

As these excuses are sincerely believed, the addict becomes increasingly separated from reality. Usually an intense crisis, such as arrest or divorce, is necessary to shake the addict from this delusional system. When there is no one in the addict's life who is either aware, concerned, or courageous enough to initiate such a crisis, the problem usually escalates.

The addict becomes an incredibly effective manipulator, largely because he learns to believe his own lies. In Steve's case, Ann occasionally became suspicious. Sometimes when she phoned the office he would be gone for hours without explanation. Several times, the money spent for gas would far exceed the amount they'd budgeted. When Ann confronted Steve, he would come up with an elaborate, detailed story. If she expressed any doubt at all, Steve would become angry. He had convinced himself that she would doubt him even if he were honest, therefore it was her problem.

He responded to her questioning by accusing her of something. When she would explain herself, Steve would compare his excuse with hers and accuse her of being paranoid. Since this had the ring of truth, Ann would begin to feel a little crazy and end up apologizing. Steve would then be convinced that his wife had a problem.

With each step in this process, Steve felt increasingly mistreated and misjudged. His focus would shift from what was being said to what he felt, which further distorted reality. Since he felt unjustly accused and he acted innocent, it followed that Ann was being unreasonable and therefore had the problem. Her apology became his proof.

Steve's case was typical in that he projected blame onto others. To be able to continue in the addiction the addict must find ways, however delusional, to attribute his problems to others. When an addict loses his job due to co-workers' complaints, the excuse is that the boss didn't like him or that business was slow. When an addict contracts a sexually transmitted disease, it's no big deal because "everyone gets it sometime." When a relationship breaks up because of his inappropriate sexual behavior, it's because "she couldn't handle the relationship."

In the same way, compulsive masturbation, pornography, prostitution, exhibitionism and dozens of other dysfunctional preoccupations become rationalized as normal and healthy. The problem escalates until a crisis occurs which cannot be rationalized away by the addict.

The problem has been described well by recovering sexual addicts. The following description has been taken from a publication of Sexaholics Anonymous, an organization of support groups for recovering sexual addicts:

> Many of us felt inadequate, unworthy, alone, and afraid. Our insides never matched what we saw on the outsides of others.

Early on, we came to feel disconnected—from parents, from peers, from ourselves. We tuned out with fantasy and masturbation. We plugged in by drinking in the pictures, the images, and pursuing the objects of our fantasies. We lusted and wanted to be lusted after.

We became true addicts: sex with self, promiscuity, adultery, dependency relationships, and more fantasy. We got it through the eyes; we bought it, we sold it, we traded it, we gave it away. We were addicted to the intrigue, the tease, the forbidden. The only way we knew to be free of it was to do it. "Please connect with me and make me whole!" we cried with outstretched arms. Lusting after the Big Fix, we gave away our power to others.

This produced guilt, self-hatred, remorse, emptiness, and pain, and we were driven ever inward, away from reality, away from love, lost inside ourselves.

Our habit made true intimacy impossible. We could never know real union with another because we were addicted to the unreal. We went for the "chemistry," the connection that had the magic, *because* it by-passed intimacy and true union. Fantasy corrupted the real; lust killed love.

First addicts, then love-cripples, we took from others to fill up what was lacking in ourselves. Conning ourselves time and again that the next one would save us, we were really losing our lives. (From *Sexaholics Anonymous* copyright 1985 by S.A. Literature. Reprinted by permission.)

BASIC MISBELIEFS

The root of the addictive system lies in a series of false beliefs that are held by the addict. These false assumptions drive him or her toward preoccupation with sex. Each misbelief reflects the addict's self-concept and leads him to his distortion of reality. The four basic false beliefs are:

1. I am basically a bad, unworthy person.
2. No one would love me as I am.
3. My needs will never be met by others.
4. My most important need is sex.

Each of these beliefs is rooted in the addict's early years of family life. These roots reach back into confused messages and lies about love, acceptance, and self-worth from parents, peers, and significant others. To discuss these roots is beyond the scope of this book. Recommendations are made in the bibliography for further reading on this topic. It will suffice for our purposes to point out that basic self-condemnation and distrust of relationships begins the cycle of impaired thinking that promotes sexual addiction. The resulting compulsive behavior in turn strengthens these beliefs. The process develops as follows:

The first belief, *I am basically a bad, unworthy person,* is the core of these individuals' self-concepts. They view themselves as inadequate failures who expect defeat. Most of these people have developed a "mask" of appropriate behavior to hide their deep feelings of worthlessness. They will go to great lengths to hide these feelings from others, due to their second belief.

No one would love me as I am. This belief isolates the addict. It becomes very important to hide fears and insecurities in order to avoid rejection and abandonment. Though they inwardly assume blame and guilt for anything that goes wrong (based on the first belief), they aren't free to take much blame or express remorse for fear of rejection. It therefore becomes impossible to be emotionally close to another person. They often portray an image of never being wrong or vulnerable in any way.

This image further isolates them from close relationships.

The third belief, *My needs will never be met by others,* is the "fuel" for the addiction. Since the addict is convinced that he is unlovable, it naturally follows that his needs for nurturance, acceptance, and love will not be met by others. He must therefore meet these needs alone. He cannot be relaxed and trusting in a relationship since he is totally responsible for his own nurturance. Consequently he becomes manipulative and controlling. The irony is that he must appear unselfish, moral, and benevolent in order to avoid rejection. At the same time he must selfishly manipulate people into meeting his needs. The addict becomes the master of the double life. What he experiences internally and what he expresses externally become increasingly incongruent. His fear of discovery develops into a growing paranoia.

The fourth belief serves to focus this tension in the direction of sexual expression: *Sex is my most important need.* In childhood the addict began a search for something to relieve the pain of unfulfilled emotional needs. Sexual sensations were discovered as something within his control which temporarily soothed emotional pain. In this way love, acceptance, and nurturance became translated into sex. The sexual addict is extremely afraid of living without sex since that would mean living without love and care. Since he is solely responsible for getting this need met, he is obsessed with sex.

The outcome of these false beliefs is addiction. The first three beliefs result in negative feelings of despair and loss of control. When an addict is sexual in some way, there is a pleasant sensation (release) followed by feelings of intense guilt. This guilt reinforces the first three false beliefs and drives the addict toward further sexual behavior. The addict says, "If these are true, I can't change it." The last belief gives a feeling of control, in that he feels he can control the meeting of his sexual need. Masturbation, sexual relationships, and visiting prostitutes are methods of controlling, all of which the addict feels guilty about.

A paradox emerges. Sexual activity never actually meets these needs but the addict believes it does. The result is an intensification and acceleration of the sexual behaviors that presumably will meet these needs. This intensification can be divided into three levels of sexual behaviors.

LEVELS OF ADDICTIVE BEHAVIOR

It is important to realize that the behaviors discussed here are not automatically an indication of sexual addiction. Many people show inappropriate sexual behavior, but they are not necessarily addicts. Others practice sexual behaviors which they regret and yet continue. They are not necessarily addicts. The addict is one whose life is out of control because of constant preoccupation with sexual activity. The addict is not simply a person with a sexual problem, he or she is a person with a sexual obsession.

It is also important to note that addiction at one of the following levels does not necessarily predict a progression to the next level. There are addicts who practice only level-one behaviors and never progress to more serious activities. The commonality among addicts is that the behavior is compulsively out of control. The sexual behavior has become the focus of the addict's daily routine, despite any risks involved. Many marriages, families, and even lives have been ruined by compulsive level-one behavior.

While a person addicted at level one may never progress to levels two or three, it is very doubtful that the opposite is true. An addict at levels two or three inevitably was compulsive at level one. In this sense the levels represent a progression.

Level-one behaviors are either not classified as illegal, or are referred to as "victimless crimes." Our society has decided they are tolerable, and in some sectors, even normal. They are behaviors which easily become compulsive and are the foundation of the sexual crimes of levels two and three.

These behaviors include compulsive masturbation, prostitution, pornography, homosexuality, and extramarital affairs. Level-one behaviors may also include heterosexual relationships that are compulsively sexual in nature. Chronic selfish sexual demands that are distasteful or insensitive to the partner may also be included at level one. Generally, an addict is not limited to any one particular behavior but is involved in many.

Level-two behaviors are clearly illegal and involve a victim. The possible consequences of getting caught become part of the excitement of sexual arousal. Although our legal system forbids these activities, our society generally views the offenders with pity. They are seen as a nuisance rather than a threat. The legal penalties are relatively minor. While there are clearly victims of these crimes, there is no physical harm inflicted. These behaviors include exhibitionism, voyeurism, obscene phone calls, and indecent liberties—touching another person in an intimate manner without his or her consent.

Level-three behaviors are serious crimes. Damage and injury to the victim is significant. Though leniency may be practiced within the legal system in some of these cases, this is certainly not the accepted attitude. In general, our society has little patience for offenders in this category. They are significant crimes with profound consequences. Included are child molestation, incest, rape, and violence.

RECOGNIZING EARLY STAGES

How can an individual recognize the potential of sexual compulsiveness as it is developing? The difficulty here is that so much of the compulsion is internal. It therefore requires that an individual be honest with himself and fight off the tendency toward denial. An individual who can do this has the potential to deal with sexual compulsion before it reaches an addictive stage; many people cannot. The following are guidelines for self-evaluating compulsive behavior:

1. Sexual behavior is used to change one's mood rather than to express intimate affection. When the purpose of sex is to avoid negative feelings, or when it becomes a source of painful feelings, it is a sign of the addictive process.

2. The sexual behavior creates pain or problems for the individual or others. Degrading oneself or exploiting others is a symptom of sexual addiction.

3. The behavior has to be kept secret. Behavior that cannot be shared with another individual indicates guilt and shame and leads to a double life.

4. The relationships involved are devoid of genuine concern or commitment. This is because the addict uses sex to avoid genuine relationship.

Fundamental to the whole concept of addiction and recovery is the healthy dimension of human relationships. The addict runs a great risk by being sexual outside of a committed relationship.

These are warning signs. They indicate escalating sexual compulsiveness. They are only helpful to the individual who is willing to be painfully honest with himself.

IS MY PARTNER AN ADDICT?

I can hear people asking this question already. It is

a valid question and deserves some straight answers. Here are some "signals" that could indicate an addiction or a dangerous obsession. None of these warning signs should be taken lightly.

When you continually feel sexually taken advantage of by your partner, these feelings, regardless of how either of you justify them, are a danger signal. They indicate an imbalance in the relationship. When you realize that you are compromising your own values or you are sacrificing important parts of the relationship for the sake of your partner's sexual satisfaction, that is another important signal. It indicates that the relationship is one-sided and that sex is the primary issue.

It is important to share these feelings of being used or being taken advantage of with your partner. If these feelings are minimized or discounted, it's an indication that your emotional needs are seen as insignificant compared to your partner's physical needs. At this point it becomes clear that the relationship is being exchanged for sex. Significant changes need to be made in order to have a healthy relationship.

Other warning signs: chronic lies about relationships or questionable behavior; constant justification or rationalization of sexual behavior that seems inappropriate; activities that always seem to be directed toward sexually compromising or seductive situations.

All of these signals revolve around the symptoms of sexual addiction. If these signals are present, with or without actual addiction, they are clear indications of a very unhealthy relationship.

Is There Hope?

As bleak and despairing as this picture may seem, there is hope for the sexual addict. There is forgiveness and healing in a union with God at the Cross. There are caring people who are available to help. There are also other sexual addicts who have overcome their compulsion and want to share their victory with others who suffer. But the individual addict must take the first step and that is where the primary difficulty lies.

Denial, rationalization, and secrecy are an intricate part of this disorder. It's a sad fact that most addicts will not understand the depth of their problem until life falls apart. Arrest, divorce, abandonment, injury, and job loss are crises that motivate an addict to search for recovery.

There is an irony in the close relationships of the addict. Those closest to the addict often do the most harm in their attempt to help. The spouse, parents, and friends unwittingly protect the addict from disaster. They often justify, excuse, deny, and lie for the addict in order to protect him from the consequences of his behavior. They may choose not to confront inappropriate behavior. They repeatedly accept shaky excuses for irresponsible actions and broken commitments. They provide alibis to employers, children, and others who experience the consequences of the addict's behavior. By preventing a crisis they take away his main motivation for change. This only perpetuates the problem by helping the addict hold onto an illusion of normalcy. Until the addict can feel the full impact of his actions, chances are slim that he will seek help. Removing the protective support is the most difficult yet important action a loved one can take.

The first step toward recovery for the addict is to admit his helplessness and then to seek help. The recovery process for the addict revolves around acknowledging and understanding the four basic misbeliefs mentioned earlier that destroy reality. Feelings of worthlessness and abandonment need to be explored. Fear of trust and vulnerability need to be resolved so that healthy relationships can be established. False beliefs must be replaced by healthy, realistic ones. New patterns of relating to others must be learned. All of this cannot be accomplished by the addict alone. His recovery will depend on support from others.

Essential to the recovery of the sexual addict is participation in a support group. There must be a commitment to those who are interested in growth and recovery. In such a group there can be mutual support and empathy while each person is held accountable for his own behavior. These groups are based on an adaptation of the "Twelve Steps" of Alcoholics Anonymous and have been developing for the past ten years across the U.S., Europe, and Canada.

Through these "Twelve Steps" the individual comes to acknowledge that the problem is more powerful than he is. He has become powerless over his addiction to lust. He must develop a faith in and dependence on God to overcome his compulsion. The source of the addict's life and self-worth must be God, rather than the addiction. He must develop healthy, trusting relationship patterns within the group context and take responsibility for his actions past, present, and future. The process is slow and painful, but the results are positive.

When an individual is willing to seek help for his compulsion there are many resources available. There are professionals who specialize in working with compulsive behavior, and there are many support groups which focus on resolving sexual addiction.

At this point the literature available on sexual addiction is very limited, although it is growing. Material is available through the organization of Sexaholics Anonymous. For literature and for information concerning support groups in your area, you may write to Sexaholics Anonymous headquarters:

S.A.
P.O. Box 300
Simi Valley, CA 93062

Other recommended books:

Claire W., *God, Help Me Stop* (P.O. Box 27364, San Diego, Calif., 1982). An independently published workbook for compulsive behaviors.

Grateful Members, *The Twelve Steps for Everyone* (Minneapolis, Minn.: CompCare Publications, 1975).

The following test was developed by Sexaholics Anonymous to help an individual evaluate his or her tendency toward sexual addiction.

1. Have you ever thought you needed help for your sexual thinking or behavior?

2. Have you thought that you'd be better off if you didn't keep "giving in"?

3. Have you thought that sex or sexual stimuli are controlling you?

4. Have you ever tried to stop or limit doing what you felt was wrong in your sexual behavior?

5. Do you resort to sex to escape, relieve anxiety, or because you can't cope?

6. Do you feel guilt, remorse, or depression afterwards?

7. Has your pursuit of sex become more compulsive?

8. Does it interfere with relations with your spouse?

9. Do you have to resort to images or memories during sex?

10. Does an irresistible impulse arise when the other party makes the overture or sex is offered?

11. Do you keep going from one "relationship" or lover to another?

12. Do you feel the "right relationship" would help you stop lusting, masturbating, or being so promiscuous?

13. Do you have a destructive need—a desperate sexual or emotional need for someone?

14. Does pursuit of sex make you careless for yourself or the welfare of your family or others?

15. Has your effectiveness or concentration decreased as sex has become more compulsive?

16. Do you lose time from work because of it?

17. Do you turn to a lower environment when pursuing sex?

18. Do you want to get away from the sex partner as soon as possible after the act?

19. Although your spouse is sexually compatible, do you still masturbate or have sex with others?

20. Have you ever been arrested for a sex-related offense?[20]

*Every [sexual] restriction in Scripture
can be summed up in one precept: Sex
should be kept within marriage.*

8

THE GENIUS
OF SCRIPTURE

"I 've been a Christian for thirteen years and I never knew the Bible said all that about sex." Marv was discussing his Bible class on sexuality and sexual expression. "I began this class expecting what I've always heard since I was a kid, all the 'Thou shalt nots'... I'm really amazed!" With a wink he added, "I'm discovering that God has a much better understanding of sex than I gave him credit for."

Our world is full of beautiful things that God has created and mankind has misused. Look at the shores of Lake Erie or the atmosphere of Los Angeles. Think of a piece of wood that can be used to build a house or to beat a man to death. Man's imagination can be exquisitely creative or profoundly destructive. So it is with the gift of our sexuality. The beauty, excitement, and security of that expression of intimacy and trust is often perverted into a selfish, manipulative demand.

One of the dangers of this two-sided coin is to project preconceived ideas onto God. Bits and pieces of Scripture are read to find only the message that is assumed to be there. Many people are like Marv. They already "know" what the Bible says. Their parents told them. The pastor told them. It fits with what they "know" the rest of the Bible says. But they've never taken the time to really get into The Book. The result is that they end up getting everyone's opinion except God's.

In this chapter, we're going to examine the biblical view of sex. This is not meant to be an exhaustive Bible study; my goal is to crack open the door and encourage you to step into your own study of the topic. If you've never before studied Scripture regarding sexuality, you may be surprised at what you find.

In a previous chapter we discussed what the book of Genesis tells us about God's view of sex. Let's look a little further and see what we find.

The Song of Solomon is an excellent illustration of God's attitude toward sexual expression. If you can get past the Hebrew symbolism, the message of the book is loud and clear. Here the young bride is describing her husband:

> *Like an apple tree among the trees of the forest*
> *is my lover among the young men.*
> *I delight to sit in his shade,*
> *and his fruit is sweet to my taste.*
> *He has taken me to the banquet hall,*
> *and his banner over me is love.*
> *Strengthen me with raisins,*
> *refresh me with apples,*
> *for I am faint with love.*
> *His left arm is under my head,*
> *and his right arm embraces me.*
> (Song of Solomon 2:3-6)

Then the groom reflects on his bride:

> *Your neck is like the tower of David,*
> *built with elegance;*
> *on it hang a thousand shields,*
> *all of them shields of warriors.*
> *Your two breasts are like two fawns,*
> *like twin fawns of a gazelle*
> *that browse among the lilies.*
> *Until the day breaks*
> *and the shadows flee,*
> *I will go to the mountain of myrrh*
> *and to the hill of incense.*
> *All beautiful you are, my darling;*
> *there is no flaw in you.*
>
> (4:4-7)

When speaking to his bride, the groom says:

> *You are a garden locked up, my sister, my bride;*
> *you are a spring enclosed, a sealed fountain.*
> *Your plants are an orchard of pomegranates*
> *with choice fruits . . . and all the finest spices.*
>
> (4:12-14)

To which his bride replies:

> *Awake, north wind,*
> *and come, south wind!*
> *Blow on my garden,*
> *that its fragrance may spread abroad.*
> *Let my lover come into his garden*
> *and taste its choice fruits.*
>
> (4:16)

Throughout the book the picture is of open, relaxed, fulfilling lovemaking between a young bride and groom who are free from guilt. Later in this chapter we'll come back to some of these passages and look at why there is freedom from guilt.

SCRIPTURAL WARNINGS

Hebrews 13:4 is an interesting verse:

Marriage should be honored by all, and the marriage bed kept pure, for God will judge the adulterer and all the sexually immoral.

The Greek term translated as "bed" in this verse is the word *koite*. It is derived from the Latin word *cotio* which gives us our English term *coitus,* meaning sexual intercourse. This exact same word, in Romans 13:13 is translated "sexual indulgence and promiscuity." The message here is that sexual indulgence is promoted within marriage. Any negative reference to this term revolves around premarital sex (fornication) or extra-marital sex (adultery). This is how the "marriage bed" is defiled; there is no other way.

First Timothy 4:4 tells us that everything God created is good. However, everything is capable of being used for either good or evil purposes. The proper use of the good gift of sex is very clear: Sex is promoted and encouraged within the stability of a marriage commitment, never outside of it. Within the loving marriage commitment, God gives no sexual restrictions at all.

The first nine chapters of Proverbs have a great deal to say about sexual expression. Chapter 5:15-21 captures the message well. This is a message of instruction from father to son, from history's wisest king to his adolescent prince. The topic is the proper use of the sex drive. Solomon uses very picturesque language.

*Drink water from your own cistern,
    running water from your own well.*

Should your springs overflow in the streets,
your streams of water in the public squares?
Let them be yours alone,
never to be shared with strangers.
May your fountain be blessed,
and may you rejoice in the wife of your youth.
A loving doe, a graceful deer—
may her breasts satisfy you always,
may you ever be captivated by her love.
Why be captivated, my son, by an adulteress?
Why embrace the bosom of another man's
wife?
For a man's ways are in full view of the Lord.
and he examines all his paths.

(Proverbs 5:15-21)

In verses 15-17 he's not talking about giving water to his neighbor's sheep! He's talking about enjoying sex with his wife. Verses 18-19 make this very clear. Sex is to be fully and luxuriously enjoyed . . . within the bounds of a lifetime commitment with one partner.

If we go back to the beginning of the chapter, we can see the concern of the king for his son and the reason behind his writing these instructions. He writes with the insight of "one who's been there":

My son, pay attention to my wisdom,
listen well to my words of insight,
that you may maintain discretion
and your lips may preserve knowledge.
For the lips of an adulteress drip honey,
and her speech is smoother than oil;
but in the end she is bitter as gall,
sharp as a double-edged sword.
Her feet go down to death;
her steps lead straight to the grave.
She gives no thought to the way of life;
her paths are crooked, but she knows it not.

Now then, my sons, listen to me;
  do not turn aside from what I say.
Keep to a path far from her,
  do not go near the door of her house,
lest you give your best strength to others
  and your years to one who is cruel,
lest strangers feast on your wealth
  and your toil enrich another man's house.
At the end of your life you will groan,
  when your flesh and body are spent.
(Proverbs 5:1-11)

Turn back a few books to Leviticus and Deuteronomy—the law given to the Israelites by God. At the time these were written, God was preparing the nation of Israel for a special task. He was going to use them to bring the Messiah to the world. His goal was to make them a successful and powerful nation. God knew that lax sexual standards would be disastrous to a society's development. He had a very effective method of discouraging promiscuity among young people. The rules went like this:

1. To begin with, all adultery was punishable by the death of both the man and the woman (Leviticus 20:10).

2. If a woman had intercourse prior to marriage and this fact was exposed on her wedding night, evidenced by the lack of a bloody sheet, she was to be executed (Deuteronomy 22:13-21).

3. If a man had sex with an engaged woman, he would be stoned to death (Deuteronomy 22:23-27).

4. If a man had intercourse with an unengaged virgin, he was forced to marry her, which included paying a dowry to her father (Deuteronomy 22:28-29).

Think about those four laws for a moment. The penalties may be severe, but they were a great method for promoting sexual accountability! We could assume that any woman who had lost her virginity prior to marriage would certainly not let the man involved get away with it. If she did, marriage to anyone else would mean the death sentence for her. If she never married there was no place for her in Hebrew society, other than perhaps the life of a harlot. All in all, it sounds like a pretty effective method of insuring sexually pure courtships. This serves to illustrate for us the high value God places on sexual abstinence outside of marriage.

Let's turn back to the Song of Solomon again. As we pointed out earlier, this is a very explicit book concerning the joys of married love. The book revolves around the relationship between Solomon and his bride, Shulamith, both before and after their wedding. Included are their sexual experiences as well as dreams, fears, and fantasies. (For a thorough discussion and commentary on this book, I recommend reading *Solomon on Sex* by Joseph Dillow.)

There is a phrase that is repeated by the bride three times: "Do not arouse or awaken love until it so desires" (2:7, 3:5, and 8:4). This phrase is primarily a warning against premarital sexual promiscuity. Its warning goes beyond that, however, and includes the arousal and excitement of sexual feelings for anyone but a committed life partner. That's an interesting statement for a discourse on sexual freedom.

The quote is found in the midst of love scenes. In these love scenes the bride is describing the beautiful, liberating experience of their love on the wedding night. She relates that beauty and freedom to their premarital chastity. The message is that sexual involvement before the wedding may endanger the beauty of sex in marriage. This puts the book into a moral context that is consistent with all of Scripture.

Considering the negative reputation the Bible has had regarding sexual issues, it is very significant to note that every restriction in Scripture can be summed up in one precept: Sex should be kept within marriage. If you have one sexual partner and you are committed to him or her for life within marriage, relax and enjoy one another in love.

While the limitations are few, the warnings are powerful. God obviously places an extremely high premium on sexual purity. As discussed earlier, the Old Testament prescribed death as a resolution for sexual promiscuity. The New Testament also has some significant statements about the dangers of sexual indiscretions. The sexual standard in the New Testament is crystal clear: No premarital sex. It makes no distinction between casual sex, recreational sex, or sex between people who are "married in God's eyes." He leaves no room for such rationalizing or justifying. Let's take a closer look at the New Testament message.

In the Greek text, the word for both fornication and immorality is *porneia*. Porneia refers to sexual activity outside the bonds of marriage. It includes premarital sex, extramarital sex, homosexuality and the whole gamut of sexual perversions. It is such a serious distortion of God's desire and plan that Christians are admonished to not only avoid any form of fornication (1 Thessalonians 4:3) but to not even talk about it (Ephesians 5:3).

I won't take the space here to quote each of the passages listed. I urge you to look them up and read them in their context. My comments will make much more sense that way.

First Corinthians 5:9-13 - Paul warned the Corinthian church not to tolerate individuals who continually practiced *porneia*, but to ostracize them in judgment.

First Corinthians 6:13-20 - The focus here is on the seriousness of illicit sexual intercourse because of its effects, both physically and spiritually. He uses the example of a harlot, but his focus is on the act, not who it's committed with. He could just as easily have referred to a co-worker or a campus cheerleader.

First Corinthians 10:8-13 - Paul explains that God dealt severely with sexual immorality in the Old Testament as an example for us who live in the last days. Verse 13 is a promise that God will not allow us to be overwhelmed by temptation. When God asks us to do something, He also guarantees that we are capable of doing it.

Galatians 5:16-21 - Illicit sexual intercourse is listed first among deeds that are diametrically opposed to the Spirit of God in a Christian's life. This passage is followed by the fruits of the Spirit, the first of which is love. The implication here may be that premarital sex as well as adultery, is the opposite of love. Verse 21 states clearly that the practice of these acts keeps people from the Kingdom of God. This is a warning that Paul repeats in 1 Corinthians 6:9-10 and Ephesians 5:5-6.

Colossians 3:5-6 - Paul assures us that the wrath of God will come as a result of porneia.

First Thessalonians 4:1-8 - Paul warns that illicit sexual intercourse is the opposite of the will of God and that God is the avenger of sexual immorality.

CONCLUSION

The story line of an Alfred Hitchcock TV episode illustrates a very important point about life. The story begins with a woman who was found guilty of murder and sentenced to life imprisonment without parole. She vowed to escape her incarceration in any way possible and was constantly in search of a foolproof plan to gain her freedom.

During her imprisonment she became friends with the prison mortician, an elderly man with a chronic and severe health problem. It was this man's job to dispose of the remains of all inmates who died in prison. He built the casket, dug the grave, saw that the casket was buried; he did it all.

The woman assured the mortician that she could find and finance a complete cure for his painful ailment if only she could be free of the prison walls. She eventually convinced the mortician to help her escape in exchange for his cure.

The plan was that when the next funeral bell tolled, announcing the death of a prisoner, the woman would find her way to the morgue and climb into the casket with the corpse. The mortician would go about his normal duties of taking the casket outside the prison and burying it in the cemetery. Within a short period of time he would return and unearth the casket and free the woman. It was an impressive plan with great potential for success.

The plan went exactly as anticipated. The bell tolled, the woman went to the morgue and entered the dark casket with the newly deceased remains. She felt the casket being moved to the graveside, lowered into the ground, and covered with dirt. She waited and waited and waited; no mortician. It seemed like an eternity before, in desperation, she ventured to strike a match to determine the time elapsed in her waiting. In the light of the small flame she made a startling discovery. The body in the casket with her was that of her mortician friend.

Can you just imagine the desperation and regret of this woman? The perfect plan. One single "hitch." Complete disaster.

So it is when we choose to ignore God's clear warnings to us in His Word. He has not given us a set of constraints . . . a set of rules and expectations that imprison us. Rather, He has lovingly provided a design for sexual fulfillment that frees us to intimately know another and be known by another. When we go our own way, all the plans, rationalizations, and excuses in the world will not change the results of violating His natural order.

The experiences shared in this book as well as the patterns and problems discussed are all predictable, expected consequences of violating the purpose of the sexual relationship. God has blessed the human race with the capability to relate sexually. His purpose is pleasure, fulfillment, and closeness, as well as procreation. We can experience great joy and fulfillment by following God's design for sexual expression, or we can misuse His gift and suffer the consequences. The choice is ours.

GROWING CLOSER

1) Look up and read 1 Thessalonians 4:1-8. Using this passage as a foundation, can you think of any good reason for having premarital sex?

2) In your own words, how is God's love expressed through the scriptural restrictions on sexual expression?

Healthy, growing, fulfilling relationships don't happen by accident. They are the result of decisions.

9

DISENGAGING
THE TRAPS

So far we've talked about the whys and wherefores, sociological and psychological problems, and the theological implications of sexual promiscuity. However, when all is said and done, we have to get back to the very real question of how we make it practical. What can a couple do today that will get them back on the right track or keep problems from beginning?

We are all aware that our society, especially the media—movies, television, music, magazines, books—constantly pump us full of sexually arousing material. We can't watch an evening of TV or thumb through a magazine without being confronted with sexual messages in a hundred different ways. It's difficult *not* to get preoccupied with sex! The message we receive is that sexual liberties without commitment are no big deal. Traditional, biblical values are nonsense. Sex is considered casual, recreational, and without moral implications one way or another. Besides, sex feels good. The sensation of arousal is pleasant, so our bodies propel us towards the very actions that cause such deep and complex problems.

Contrary to popular belief, we do not have to be driven to action by these impulses. They may be natural and normal, but it's a myth that they are overpowering or irresistible. We choose how we allow them to affect us, and we choose our behavior in response to them. Dr. Sol Gorden gives an excellent illustration of this capacity. Picture two teenagers on the couch passionately necking and getting more and more involved. At one point the boy says "I've got to go for it! I can't help myself! There's no stopping it!" The girl only needs to say, "I think I hear my mother coming," and that young man will suddenly find a way to stop! It's amazing.

As the Christian single develops a standard of sexual expression, the issues discussed in this book become extremely relevant. It's clear that Scripture says chastity is a requisite of Christian singleness, and that the consequences of disobedience can be severe. God has not only given us the responsibility to live within these limits, He created us with the ability to do so. For the sincere individual or couple who wants their physical relationship to progress in a biblical, healthy, realistic way, there is a great deal of hope.

TEN STEPS TO SUCCESS

Preparing for a lifetime commitment is an extensive process. It takes much time and effort. Unfortunately, most people spend more time preparing to get a driver's license than preparing for marriage! The following suggestions regarding sexual development are applicable to any couple who want to maintain or regain sexual purity.

1. *If you have been sexually active as a couple, agree that it is a problem and that it will damage your relationship.* Regard-

less of the justification for the sexual relationship, it's important that each of you asks forgiveness of one another and of God. By verbalizing your regrets and mistakes, this particular conversation becomes a "marker" for the turning point of your relationship. It will also help you become accountable to one another for the development of your relationship. Commit yourselves to making a change in this area.

2. *Avoid sexually stimulating material.* This includes pornographic films or literature, and openly suggestive television programs or music. Beware of anything that artificially stimulates sexual desire. These examples may seem innocent or even trite, but exposing yourself to their influence lowers motivation to remain pure and leads to compromising of values. By staying away from stimulation as individuals, couples will find it much easier to avoid temptation as a unit.

3. *Spend time in material that is positive and strengthens biblical values.* There is no substitute for reading and meditating on Scripture. There are also countless good books and cassette tapes that can replace the negative sexual input we encounter daily. You may have some favorite inspirational speakers or writers. If not, your pastor or local Christian bookstore may have some suggestions.

There is a saying among computer programmers that is true for everyone: "Garbage in . . . garbage out." We can choose what we allow to fill our minds, and what our minds are filled with will control our behavior. "For as [a man] thinks within himself, so he is" (Proverbs 23:7, NASB).

4. *Avoid purposely or consciously escalating sexual arousal in one another.* Ask the question, "Can I morally satisfy the desires I'm arousing in this person?" If you cannot (and you cannot if you are not married to that person),

then the arousal of your partner's passion is a type of defrauding. The normal, healthy emotional development of the loving relationship you really desire is stifled, and the "traps" discussed throughout this book are being baited and set.

5. *Sit down together and honestly discuss your beliefs, hopes, and fears, and your desires regarding your physical relationship.* Be specific as you talk about what puts each of you in the danger zone. This will take a great deal of honesty and vulnerability. You cannot control sexual urges by denying them. You will need to discuss them and develop a plan. Don't pretend you don't enjoy sex if you do enjoy it. Admit the potential for serious problems and make some mutual decisions about handling temptation. Your ability and willingness to communicate on this level will tell you a great deal about your readiness for marriage. If you or your partner cannot or will not do this, it's a signal that the relationship needs a great deal of development before marriage. By discussing it as a couple, you both take responsibility for this part of the relationship. Neither partner should get away with saying, "You stop me." Only a team effort will strengthen intimacy and communication.

6. *Decide together on a level of physical involvement that promotes and develops genuine communication in the relationship.* Go with the more conservative view. This means if you are comfortable with long periods of kissing in a parked car, and your partner prefers no more than a goodnight kiss on the porch, the limit should be set as a goodnight kiss on the porch. Otherwise, there still will be the struggle with guilt, and the potential for developing illicitness. One of you may feel "used" by the other and start resenting it. Beware of a partner who attempts to coerce you into deeper levels of involvement than are comfortable. The concern may be more for self-gratification than for developing a healthy, mutually satis-

fying relationship. In this case, marriage plans are probably premature.

7. *Discuss whether there may be certain times, places, or situations that predictably lead one or both of you into temptation in this area.* You may discover that either or both of you are more easily tempted because of a particular situation such as being alone in a parked car at night or lying down together. It is important that you both know your areas of temptation and discuss them together as specifically as possible. Exploring these specifics together will help you find and agree upon the limits of your physical relationship. This will require honest communication and creativity, skills which are essential in a healthy marriage. The following are examples from my case files of specific limits different couples have agreed on.

NO KISSING UNLESS WE ARE STANDING UP. This couple decided that temptation became too strong when they sat or lay down while kissing.

NO PHYSICAL CONTACT AFTER 10:00 P.M. This couple discovered that temptation was greatest late at night when they were tired and their motivation to resist was low.

NO REMOVAL OF ANY CLOTHING. This couple felt comfortable with the agreement that the first button, zipper, or snap that was undone or opened signaled that the boundaries had been crossed and they needed to separate for a time.

STAY OFF THE COUCH WHEN WE'RE ALONE. This couple found that the couch in either of their apartments was the place of greatest temptation, so they decided to sit elsewhere when they were alone together.

Set the boundaries early enough in the arousal process so that you both agree it is realistic to stop. If your plan is to get as involved and excited as you possibly can and then back off at the last minute, you're probably being unrealistic and will end up with regrets. It's important that you establish your goals and priorities *before* you are tempted. The time to look for a bomb shelter is before the enemy attacks.

The importance of taking these steps *as a couple* is illustrated by Dr. Dwight Carlson:

> It's like driving 90 mph down a city street and a child runs out in front of the car. We may jam on the brakes and have every intention of stopping, but the actual decision was made when we chose to go 90 mph on a city street. Once that decision is made, it's sometimes very difficult to reverse.
>
> The same holds true in sexual temptation: The amount of physical contact and the setting a couple place themselves in are important factors in avoiding temptations. So the guidelines have to be drawn early enough so as not to get so excited and so involved sexually that they reach a point that it's difficult if not impossible to stop."[21]

8. *Write your mutual decision down on paper.* Again, be specific. This is necessary to eliminate misunderstandings or power struggles. If both persons have verbally agreed that his hand under her blouse is "too far," and that limit has been written down, then neither individual is fooling the other. Then it's easy to recognize manipulation, impulsiveness, and selfish motivation. Writing limits together is like shining a spotlight on that area of the relationship. It will immediately become clear to both individuals when the limit becomes a problem. If it never becomes a problem, there may never be a need to discuss it again. As long as the mutual limits are respected, the couple can relax and respond freely and spontaneously, knowing that their sexual relationship is preparing them for a healthy marriage.

9. As you apply these steps to your relationship, *remember to affirm your love for one another.* It will be important to remind one another of your love regularly, especially at times when one of you is feeling insecure or distant—a time when temptation may be intensified for that person. The motivation for making these decisions is your love for your partner and your commitment to the relationship. As you eliminate sexual behavior, you'll have the need and the opportunity to increase other forms of communicating your love. Thoughtful behaviors, small and meaningful gifts, as well as verbal expressions of love will deepen in their significance.

10. *If you or your partner are continually crossing the boundaries or pushing the limits, do not ignore or minimize the implications of that behavior!* This should be a blaring signal that the relationship is not developing in the way both of you have agreed that it should develop. If you both find yourselves consciously ignoring your mutually agreed-upon standards, repeatedly putting yourselves into situations that you know will cause you trouble with temptation, then it is time to evaluate your motivation. You may need to face the fact that you are not particularly interested in the development of the relationship, but mainly in physical pleasure or gratification. Your behavior is an indication that commitment, motivation, or communication is not what it should be and will cause significant problems later on. If this is the case, all the insight, information, and strategies in the world won't help your relationship grow beyond this point. As the old saying goes, "Ya gotta wanna!"

Ask yourselves, "Are we really concerned about the relationship, or is our concern mainly for self-gratification?" Obviously, self-gratification is a totally inadequate basis for marriage. At this point you may have to agree or admit that this relationship is a poor prospect for marriage, either because of the impulsiveness of each of you or the disregard one of you has for the other's values. Whatever the reason, it is much better to discover these problems prior to the marriage and postpone or cancel the wedding plans than to set yourselves up for serious problems in marriage that will be extremely difficult and painful to resolve later.

Wherever you choose to set your limits, it will become boring and mundane if your purpose in physical contact is just to experience sexual excitement. Remember that sexual arousal is progressive, it draws you into more and more involvement. A kiss, for example, soon becomes dull if your focus is the excitement you experience by touching lips. You can prevent kissing from becoming routine if your conscious purpose is to express your feelings to your partner. A kiss will always remain meaningful if it is a form of communication rather than a method of self-gratification. Also, if your kiss is honestly an expression of love, that love will not force itself past your agreed-upon boundaries in order to feel good. First Corinthians 13:5 reminds us that true love is not self-seeking.

Remember that whatever limits you decide on as a couple, there is no one to apply them but the two of you—no parents, no teachers, no pastor, no friend—no one but you. Remember also that being accountable to one another is an extremely important skill to bring to a marriage.

I ask each couple I work with to tell me what it was like to discuss setting physical boundaries and how they see it affecting their relationship. Some say it was easy; many say it was awkward and difficult to begin. The vast majority have said that once they discussed their honest feelings and convictions and made their decisions regarding limits, their relationship became much more relaxed. Many describe it as a "turning point" in their feeling of closeness. They no longer worried about what the other was thinking. They suddenly felt much more secure and they all reported a sense of deepened intimacy without the complications of deepening their physical involvement. Never has anyone even hinted that he or she regretted having had the discussion.

Two Facts to Remember

There are two important principles underlying all that has been written here about taking steps to maintain sexual purity. First, for most individuals, the desire for sex is actually a desire for closeness and intimacy. The most sexually active single people are usually the loneliest. As we discussed in chapter 2, sex feels intimate, but since it can actually be a substitute for intimacy, it does not satisfy for long. By focusing on emotional intimacy and honest communication, you will find the tendency toward sexual compulsion decreasing.

Secondly, sex is progressive; it builds on itself. The single person or the couple who gives in to sexual temptation will find it more difficult to resist the next time. By not giving in to temptation, it becomes less and less powerful. By avoiding sexual behavior as well as sexually arousing material, sexual tension will be reduced, not increased, over time.

I Can't Imagine Feeling Clean Again

Nancy was a twenty-two-year old woman with a very serious concern. We never met. My contact with her was limited to a telephone call she made to a live radio broadcast I was doing. But Nancy represents many people. Here is what she said: "I don't know what to do now. I'd give anything to be able to just erase the last nine years of my life. After losing my virginity at thirteen, I figured, what's the difference? I've got nothing left to lose. I've gotten involved sexually whenever I felt like it and often when I didn't. Now I've had three abortions and I've slept with so many men I can't count them all. I've wanted so badly to be loved, and I'm realizing that no man has ever really loved me. Through some Christian friends, I'm learning that there is a better way, but how do I go back? I feel so dirty and used that I can't imagine feeling clean again. What can I do?"

There is hope for Nancy. There is hope for other women and men who, like Nancy, are casualties of the sexual revolution. While a person's sexual virginity can't be restored, people and situations can change. A person can minimize and even eliminate many of the patterns described in this book. It's never too late.

A person chooses whether or not his past mistakes and failures strengthen and develop his character. A person is never trapped by his past if he's willing to change. Each of us has the capability of growing and becoming stronger regardless of our experiences—sometimes because of them.

The first thing Nancy needed to understand was the issue of forgiveness. Though Nancy's behavior had caused her a multitude of problems, the Bible tells us that her sin is no worse than any other. In James 2:10-11 we are told, "For whoever keeps the whole law and yet stumbles at just one point is guilty of breaking all of it. For he who said, 'Do not commit adultery,' also said, 'Do not murder.' If you do not commit adultery, but do commit murder, you have become a lawbreaker." This may sound hopeless until one realizes that the death of Christ on the cross paid for all sins. Because of Christ's sacrifice, God offers forgiveness to everyone, regardless of the crime.

How did Jesus deal with sexual sin in others? Read the story in John 8. The woman's crime was adultery, the law required her death. After assuring her that He didn't condemn her, Christ's instruction was, "Go now and leave your life of sin." (John 8:11).

God does not become angry and reject you when you have failed. He is always holding you close and expecting success, regardless of your feelings of failure. The dangerous tendency for people like Nancy is to become preoccupied with their mistakes. But focusing on failure is no solution—it intensifies feelings of guilt and drives a person back to his problem behavior.

If you are in a similar situation to Nancy's, focus on your failure only long enough to fully understand what needs to change. Make yourself aware of early warning signs so that you'll recognize when the problem begins to recur.

Here are four steps to follow in dealing with past sexual mistakes:

1. *Agree that you have violated God's standards.* Nothing can change until you take responsibility for your part in the behavior. Call it sin; don't blame anyone else. God is not surprised. "We all, like sheep, have gone astray, each of us has turned to his own way; and the LORD has laid on him the iniquity of us all" (Isaiah 53:6).

2. *Choose to believe God's promise of forgiveness.* The penalty for your sin was paid in full at Calvary. You need only to lay claim to it. "If we confess our sins, he is faithful and just and will forgive us our sins and purify us from all unrighteousness" (1 John 1:9).

3. *Choose to forgive yourself.* Read through Romans 8 several times and think about what it says about you. Don't buy into guilt trips. If God has forgiven you, you are forgiven. Forgiving yourself means accepting your humanness and agreeing that Christ did the whole job on the cross. There is no more to add to it by your own suffering or self-pity.

4. *Decide to make a change.* This chapter has discussed methods to help you change behavior relating to the building of healthy physical relationships. Make some

145

decisions about how you will handle your relationships differently. Determine to change old patterns.

It is possible to have the relationship you desire. No matter what your past has been, your future can be different. But remember that healthy, growing, fulfilling relationships don't happen by accident. They are the result of decisions, commitment, and labor. The first decision must be made by you as an individual. If you are a single adult and desire healthy sexual patterns for yourself and your future spouse, I strongly encourage you to invest your time in the steps suggested in this chapter. Getting started may be uncomfortable, but the relationship pay-off is well worth the investment!

GROWING CLOSER

These exercises will help stimulate a more open and specific discussion of your physical relationship with your partner. Regardless of how long you have known each other, you will find that this discussion will deepen your understanding of yourself, each other, and your relationship.

1. Read and discuss 1 Thessalonians 4:3-7 together. Talk about this passage in terms of how it applies to your relationship.

2. Complete the following statements as honestly and completely as you can. Each of you should complete them separately, then discuss what each has written. When we are with others, or in public, you often _____, and when you do, I feel _____. What I would really appreciate is _____.

When we are alone and you _____, I feel _____. I would like to feel _____, and it would help me if you would _____.

At this point in our physical relationship, I feel very comfortable when we _____, but become uneasy when we _____.

When we are getting more involved than you and I have agreed we should, the most helpful thing you can do for me is _____.

147

EPILOGUE

While completing the final manuscript for this book, I met a young married couple with an encouraging story to tell. Although there are many more details than can be shared here, I include a portion of their experience because it illustrates so well the purpose of this book. I am grateful to them for allowing us to "peek in" on their experience as a couple.

Doug and Kathy met while in college. They fell in love almost immediately and were soon spending every spare moment together. Since they both assumed they would be sleeping together before long, they began to discuss and plan for their contraceptives, and went together to purchase them. They made that night as romantic as possible. Their communication was good and their goal was to do everything "correctly." That night was the enjoyable beginning of an active sex life that was satisfying to both of them.

After a number of months however, dissatisfaction began to creep in. Something just wasn't right. For some time, Doug and Kathy could escape the tension with sex. But even this area of their relationship became dissatisfying to them. They tried sexual abstinence, thinking "it'll get better if we stop for a while." They began to experience a lack of real intimacy, though neither was sure what the problem was or what to do about it.

In the midst of this confusion, Kathy was confronted with the idea that sex before marriage was "sin." Though they had no concept of Christ's forgiveness or of personal salvation, Doug and Kathy considered themselves Christians, and since neither would consider themself a hypocrite, the idea of premarital sex as sin helped confirm their decision of abstinence.

Both Doug and Kathy had attended church in childhood. In more recent years they had been involved in a variety of religious experiences from passive involvement in various churches to experimenting with the New Age movement. When they were invited to attend church by a Christian friend, both felt comfortable attending. The message of the morning was from the book of Jonah. The topic was "running from God." It was a sermon that hit both of them "right between the eyes." That evening, after a long and tearful discussion with their Christian friend, both Doug and Kathy accepted Christ as their Savior and Lord.

While their new spiritual awareness was very exciting to both of them, they still struggled with sexual desires. Now, more than ever, they were keenly aware of the fact that God wanted them to continue in sexual abstinence. They made a commitment to one another and even wrote it down together. They called it "Seven Ground Rules for Love":

1. If it doesn't please and glorify God, it has no place in our relationship; He is the head of our love.

2. When we feel the pressure building, we will put some space between us.

3. When we get too wrapped up in each other, we will turn our eyes and open our hearts to Christ.

4. Certain fondling and intimacy is reserved for the sanctity of marriage.

5. A hug will serve the purpose of communicating our love for each other.

6. We will strive to communicate the love we share, rather than our physical attraction to each other.

7. When we struggle with this, we will remember that Jesus can and will help us through if we only stop and ask him.

After writing this commitment together, both Kathy and Doug signed it and kept it where it could be referred to whenever necessary.

Maintaining their commitment was extremely difficult. There were many emotional conversations while working through insecurities, fears, and forgiveness. There were times when the emotional struggle seemed beyond their ability to handle it. Through all their difficulties, their commitment to the relationship remained strong as did their commitment to sexual purity. More than two years after their decision for sexual abstinence, Doug and Kathy married.

Not long before their wedding, they were shopping for lingerie for the wedding night. As Kathy looked at the sexy negligees, she realized she had never really enjoyed wearing them. In the past, she had bought and worn them to please Doug, but she was more comfortable in long, cozy, warm nightgowns. However, her deep desire for Doug's satisfaction kept her looking through the rack of nighties.

"Which do you like, Doug?" she asked over her shoulder.

151

"Y'know, I really don't like any of those," he replied. "Don't you think you'd be more comfortable in this one? It's more your style and I think you'd look great in it."

Kathy turned to see Doug holding a long white flannel nightgown. As tears clouded her eyes, several things became very clear to Kathy. The nightgown signified Doug's love and his understanding of her needs, while its color signified her desire for restored sexual purity. Through their commitment and frustrations of the past two years, they had become very much "in tune" with each other. They had learned to communicate in ways they had never known possible.

Their wedding night was full of discoveries. After more than two years of sexual abstinence, both found themselves extremely nervous, but were strongly reassured in their anxiety as they realized this was what a wedding night should be like. In Kathy's words, "I was nervous and I *loved* it!"

Kathy made another discovery on the wedding night. Her previous experiences of intercourse had never resulted in orgasm. She assumed that her sexual experience was as physically fulfilling as it could possibly be. She was quite shocked and pleased to discover there was more.

Another confirming experience for them on the wedding night was that Kathy experienced the pain and light bleeding typical of a first sexual experience. Though others may disagree, Kathy is convinced this was God's assurance of her restored innocence and purity.

Doug and Kathy have no regrets regarding their premarital commitment to abstinence. In spite of their early mistakes, this couple found hope. The foundation of that hope was their desire to follow the Lord in response to their new-found salvation. Their obedience brought healing and growth to their relationship.

It is my prayer that this book can help others discover what this couple found.

NOTES

1. *Time*, 4 December 1985, p. 81. Used by permission.

2. *People*, 13 April 1987, p. 111.

3. *New Research: The Family in America*, (Rockford, Ill.: The Rockford Institute Center on the Family in America, December 1987), p. 1.

4. Helen Singer Kaplan, *The New Sex Therapy* (New York: Brunner-Mazel, 1974), p. 159.

5. Desmond Morris, *Intim.. 'e Behaviour* (New York: Random House, 1971), pp. 74-78.

6. Tim Stafford, "Love, Sex & the Whole Person," *Campus Life*, December 1987, p. 8. Used by permission.

7. Michael R. Cosby, *Sex in the Bible: An Introduction to What the Scriptures Teach Us about Sexuality* (New Jersey: Prentice-Hall, 1984), pp. 172, 176.

8. Josh McDowell, *Why Wait?* (San Bernardino, Calif.: Here's Life Publishers, 1987).

9. Joseph Dillow, *Solomon on Sex* (Nashville: Thomas Nelson, 1982), p. 24.

10. *Time*, 9 December 1985, p. 79. Used by permission.

11. *Practical Applications*, Center for Adolescent Mental Health, St. Louis, Mo., 3 (Winter 1986): 3.

12. *Psychology Today*, October 1987, p. 34.

13. Ibid.

14. *People*, 13 April 1987, p. 115.

15. Dr. Anne Speckhard as quoted by Josh McDowell, *Why Wait?* (San Bernardino, Calif.: Here's Life Publishers, 1987), p. 218.

16. *Campus Life*, December 1987, p. 40.

17. Ibid., p. 41.

18. Patrick Carnes, *Out of the Shadows* (Minneapolis: Comp-Care Publishers, 1983), p. 4.

19. Ibid., p. 10.

20. Sexaholics Anonymous, © 1985. Used by permission.

21. Dwight Carlson, *Sex and the Single Christian: Candid Conversations* (Ventura, Calif.: Regal Books, 1985), p. 53.